W9-DEA-577

THE
WORD
INTERPRETS
US

THE
WORD
INTERPRETS
US

Merrill R. Abbey

♫

ABINGDON PRESS
NASHVILLE • NEW YORK

THE WORD INTERPRETS US

Copyright © 1967 by Abingdon Press

Library of Congress Catalog Number: 67-11008

SET UP, PRINTED, AND BOUND BY THE
PARTHENON PRESS, AT NASHVILLE,
TENNESSEE, UNITED STATES OF AMERICA

To the memory of

Helen M. Henton

1849-1941

pioneer of the opening prairies
who strove to plant the church
and its gospel at the heart of
their life; grandmother who
gave my orphaned boyhood a
mother's love and a father's
strength; lover of the Word,
who taught me to read the
meaning of my life in its mirror

Preface

Thunderous events enforce the demand for a biblical mandate in control of preaching. Accommodation to culture brought forth Hitler's German-Christian Church as an instance, classic but not final, of proclamation adrift from biblical anchorage. Whatever the values of such messages as Norman Vincent Peale's "positive thinking," Thomas J. J. Altizer's "death of God theology," and Pierre Berton's *The Comfortable Pew,* their diversity is beyond dispute. Yet they have one common element—the unchecked innovations of a message which repudiates responsibility for scriptural validation. When the primary sources are extra-biblical, the message is subject to the vagaries, wise or wrong-headed, of the passing moment. The church of the mid-twentieth century needs a biblical message to guide its gropings for the way.

Biblical preaching, however, is only as dependable as the canons of interpretation on which it stands. The solitary witness of many a Bible passage lends sanction to acts which outrage mature moral standards and to estimates of truth which put roadblocks in the way of advancing knowledge. Even when seen in a wholeness that exorcises these evils, the message is set in a world view and couched in an idiom which must be translated before it can be believed. Biblical preaching is only as responsible and persuasive in the pulpit as has been this translation in the study.

Exciting work is now being done in the field of interpretation. Some of its insights are so fresh as to justify the title of one recent book, *The New Hermeneutic*. The present study does not seek to probe these findings in depth; its aim is more immediately "practical." Yet it draws on these insights for its approach to the week-by-week preparation of the preacher, and especially for its key concept: that the biblical message becomes God's Word to any hearer when it gets inside his mind and speaks with inner authority by showing him himself in the mirror of the divine encounter.

With no claim to either the full understanding or close agreement of a disciple, the author acknowledges his indebtedness to the writings of Gerhard Ebeling. They have enriched the chapters that follow, but their service is that of throwing fresh light on convictions and practices already formulated in a long preaching ministry. Through the tumult of a wartime ministry at the heart of a great city and the test of a dozen years at the crossroads of thought on the university campus, these methods of interpretation so met the demands of the encounter with the mind of today as to confirm the conviction that a steady diet of biblical preaching can have endless variety, moving timeliness, and power to build up the church.

In its attempt to be useful alike to seminarian and working pastor, this book follows a systematic plan. Chapters 1-3 set forth the concept of the Word that interprets *us,* in both its theological rationale and its practical significance. Chapters 4 and 5 outline a plan for making this concept come alive in a pulpit ministry rounded and cumulative in impact over extended periods, with some direct homiletic guidance to that end. The two final chapters then relate all this to two central concerns of biblical preaching: responsible Christian use of the Old Testament and the locating of the "gospel" in any text.

My many obligations to other workers in this field are recognized, so far as I am able to identify them, in footnotes throughout the text. I acknowledge here some grounds for gratitude too basic for footnotes to cover: to Andrew Blackwood, for his solid works on biblical preaching which guided my early attempts; to students and fellow ministers who, in classroom and conference, have clarified my thinking in lively discussion; to Garrett Theological Seminary and its president, Orville H. McKay, for a quarter's sabbatical leave in which the foundation draft was hammered out; and, as always, to my wife for assuming the tedious but valuable task of making the index, as well as for her patient endurance of my preoccupation and her enthusiastic support of the whole endeavor.

MERRILL R. ABBEY

Contents

1

Interpreted by the Text

LIFE IN SCRIPTURAL PERSPECTIVE

A young soldier's blunt question states one central problem of the church. Concerning the writers of the biblical documents, he demanded: "What do a bunch of camel drivers have to say to me in a jet age?" [1] Amid explosive change, the assumption loomed that, yesterday having forfeited its authority, today must supply its own standards. The youth's query underlies the more sophisticated challenge of those who fear that preaching has had its day. With the changing

---

[1] Quoted by Roy L. Honeycutt in *Crisis and Response* (Nashville: Abingdon Press, 1965), p. 105.

shape of the parish, they suggest, the pulpit is outmoded. The mass media render preaching passé. Discoveries in group dynamics deny the authenticity of the solo message; new research reveals communication as a two-way street.

To suppose that these factors invalidate preaching is to presume that new devices void the necessity of a word from beyond ourselves. Such an assumption forgets the nature of the Christian salvation. "Faith," wrote Paul, "comes from what is heard" (Rom. 10:17). It rises in response to a Word spoken. We do not derive it by our devices, however advanced. Conference, dialogue, group dynamics can play a useful role in *understanding* the Word, but their real function lies in the realm of response, not generation. Consensus cannot produce saving faith. The gospel emerges from neither personal analysis nor group interaction. Its resistant reality from beyond ourselves arrests us and sets us on a new course. Novel methods of response do not render obsolete this Word spoken to our need.

Preaching is the process by which the Word confronts us; at this point the young soldier's question is crucial. What camel drivers can say to the jet age depends finally on the nature of their relation to us. If their function is to lay down rules, declare propositions, what *can* they say to us? Rules have lost their context in a way of life long gone. Our understanding of the cosmos, our psychological interpretation of ourselves, our philsophical concepts of God are so altered as to cast propositions adrift from any fixed reference point. But suppose rules and propositions were not the charter of biblical authority. What if these men of yesterday hold the mirror to us? Technology changes, but man endures much as he has always. Individuals can be transformed, life styles

14

revolutionized, but the nature of man remains constant. Probing human experience in stark honesty at ultimate depths, the Bible shows us who we are and what our lives mean.

If it is to speak to us with this inner authority, however, scripture must be interpreted. "The text by means of the sermon," writes Gerhard Ebeling, "becomes a hermeneutic aid in the understanding of present experience." [2] "Hermeneutic" here refers to the stance we take as we interpret. In hermeneutics we examine presuppositions which, hidden or unexamined, may leave us with a skewed message of whose bias we are not aware. The hermeneutic disciplines ask basic questions: What significance has history for biblical interpretation? What is the basis of the interpreter's authority to draw what he does from the record? Since it is one thing to hear a fact and quite another to comprehend its meaning, what is the basis of understanding? Is the Bible to be read as a collection of varied documents, or as a work with an integrated message emerging from its wholeness? What, indeed, is the purpose of the Bible itself? Whatever meaning we extract from a passage will depend on our answers to these prior questions. Exegesis asks: What does the text *say?* But hermeneutics delve deeper: In the light of our whole approach to the Scriptures, what does this text *mean?*

Even more, the hermeneutic task is to interpret the meaning of contemporary experience, much as the judicial process uses case law. A present situation has reached some tangle which presents an issue to be understood and resolved. Appeal to legal precedent and past decisions clarifies the troublesome present issue. This is legal hermeneutic, which interprets the law as a means of resolving an issue in con-

[2] *Word and Faith* (Philadelphia: Fortress Press, 1963), p. 331.

temporary life.[3] Likewise, biblical hermeneutic—a prime responsibility of the pulpit—brings men of an extant age into such encounter with the Word spoken to all ages as to clarify and reshape their life in relation to the living God.

THE TEXT TURNS THE TABLES

This interpretative task stands out in clearer delineation when seen in distinction from two alternative conceptions of preaching. In one classic formulation, the role of the sermon is that of expounding the content of a passage from the Bible. "All that is required of a preacher," as Karl Barth states this directive, "is to keep to the text and confine his discourse to expounding it. . . . It is not possible, in one sermon, to discourse on a particular subject (thematic preaching) and to expound a passage of Scripture (homiletic)." [4] As often understood, this conception of preaching requires simply that the sermon say what the text has said, dealing with its main elements in consecutive order. Such preaching has the built-in handicap that men of our time are not equipped to gather current meaning from what Amos, Paul, Luke, Jesus said to the men of their day. It may be a learned exercise in antiquities, but it is not a living word to them.

Barth's own preaching, vividly and savingly alive, goes beyond this exclusive preoccupation with expounding the text, to bring the text into startling conversation with *our*

[3] Cf. the development of this metaphor by James M. Robinson in "Hermeneutic Since Barth," in *The New Hermeneutic,* James M. Robinson and John B. Cobb, Jr., eds. (New York: Harper & Row, 1964), p. 8.
[4] *The Preaching of the Gospel* (Philadelphia: The Westminster Press, 1963), pp. 43, 58.

life. For Barth's sermons reveal a hidden element not noticed in his theory. Having so defined preaching as to restrict it to an explanation of the text, he remarks somewhat incidentally that "those to whom he is going to speak must constantly be present in the mind of the preacher while he is preparing his sermon. What he knows about them will suggest unexpected ideas and associations which will be with him as he studies his text and will provide the element of actuality, the application of his text to the contemporary situation." [5] This element which gives vibrant life to Barth's own preaching is omitted from his basic *definition* and given only passing notice in his *theory.* To take the principal guidance for the preacher's preparation from the mandate simply to expound a text is to risk the hazard of losing the vitality found when preaching *interprets our life.*

It may indeed violate the essential nature of the biblical text itself. For the Bible is not primarily historical record, but personal message. Its documents arose from faith to speak to faith, which is to say: They are direct address. Obvious in the case of such communications as the New Testament epistles, this is no less true of such "salvation history" as is found in Genesis, Exodus, or Deuteronomy. The historic narrative in these documents is not set down impersonally as a dispassionate record of what transpired; it is rather the subject of faith's profound meditation, set forth in order that faith may be awakened in the reader who is addressed. Or note how form criticism shows the Gospels to be composed from material drawn from the life of the early church, including its preaching. To deal with such

[5] *Ibid.,* p. 74.

17

material exclusively by exposition of what it *has said* is to risk treating it as past record rather than as living message.

In order to let the texts speak in their own voice, as message, the interpreter must address them as a current word to persons now present, concerning their own life. As Gustaf Wingren well says, "An *exposition* does not necessitate any presupposition about the reader's or the hearer's existential situation, but it belongs to the very nature of a *message* that it must always presuppose something about the receiver. A message of liberation is sent to a prisoner." [6]

At the opposite pole from expounding the text stands what has been called "project preaching." "Every sermon," according to this conception, "should have for its main business the head-on constructive meeting of some problem which [is] puzzling minds, burdening consciences, distracting lives." [7] Such preaching has exciting strength in the immediacy of its engagement with the demanding moment at which the listener stands. In the work of Harry Emerson Fosdick it led to creative saving faith for a numberless host of his generation. With Fosdick, as with Barth, there is a hidden element in the *preaching,* too lightly passed over in the defining *theory.* Of this element Fosdick writes: "This did not mean that the Bible's importance in preaching diminished. Upon the contrary, I had been suckled on the Bible, knew it and loved it, and I could not deal with any crucial problem in thought and life without seeing text after text lift up its hands begging to be used." [8] In those who adopted the

---

[6] *The Living Word* (Philadelphia: Fortress Press, 1965), p. 71 n.

[7] Harry Emerson Fosdick, *The Living of These Days* (New York: Harper & Row, 1956), p. 94.

[8] *Ibid.,* p. 95.

method, however, this biblical orientation was not always present; the basic theory had not required it. At the end of his ministry, Dr. Fosdick himself noted that he "went through project preaching and beyond it." [9]

Three basic hazards to preaching often emerge from this method. (a) The statement of the problem can become more convincing than the answer. Vivid, colorful, specific in sketching the difficulty to be met, the sermon often lapses into flaccid generalities in its attempt to point the way out— a weakness hard to avoid when the message is rooted in no scripture as concrete and as vividly relived as was the initial problem. (b) The question can be posed in a way to make it lead to a preconceived answer. This subtle skewing detracts from the honesty of the preaching and sacrifices something of the vitality of the project method for the listener, who sees that the problem *thus* stated is not really the problem he must face. (c) The answer offered by the sermon may be so controlled by the questions men are asking as to lose some of the originality and force of what the gospel has to say.[10] If the preacher has the insight to move from the superficial questions we too often ask to the restatement on deeper levels which biblical truth demands, his ministry need not be thus betrayed; but he has no sure guide to such insight unless he takes his stand within a text which interprets our life.

To see preaching as such interpretation of us—judgment, guidance, insight born of an encounter with God through the text—will enable the preacher to build on the strengths and

[9] *Ibid.*, p. 100.
[10] These three difficulties have a close parallel in a critique of the theological method of Paul Tillich, by George Tavard, *Commonweal,* Dec. 11, 1964.

have some hope of deliverance from the weaknesses of both these methods. Holding text and current experience together, he has the authentic insight of the one and the immediate urgency of the other. He is adrift neither from biblical authority nor from the recognizable life of the man in the pew. "In dealings with the text," writes Gerhard Ebeling, "*its* being interpreted by us turns into *our* being interpreted by the text." [11]

TWO-WAY DIALOGUE WITH THE TEXT

Preaching so understood holds text and experience together in their interacting interpretative roles. The interpreter is not freed from the diligent exegetical-critical work required of the expositor who expounds a text. If the text is to interpret *us,* we must bring every resource we can to our endeavor to understand *it.* We must see its meaning illuminated by its context. We must understand what it said to the human situation in its own time, and what bearing that has on what it says to us now, by careful orientation to its historical background and the situation which called it forth.

What once was serious is still serious today, and what today is serious, and not just accidental and peripheral, stands in direct relation to what was once serious. Our questions, if we understand ourselves aright, are the questions of Paul, and Paul's answers, if their light illumines us, must be our answers. . . . The understanding of history is a continuous, increasingly open and urgent discussion between the wisdom of yesterday and the wisdom of tomorrow, which are one and the same.[12]

[11] Quoted by Robinson, "Hermeneutic Since Barth," p. 68.
[12] Karl Barth, *Romans,* quoted in *The New Hermeneutic,* pp. 22-23.

Yet we cannot suppose that this interplay will become apparent if the interpreter's attention is confined exclusively to expounding the text.

He needs also to look carefully at contemporary life. This he will do in a variety of ways. He will study the mass media for the "axioms" which men of our time take for granted, from which their thinking begins and on which their endeavors are based.[13] He will listen to novelists, playwrights, and other creative artists for their sensitive perception of our individual and social gropings. Most constantly of all, as an empathic and concerned pastor he will keep refocusing his awareness of his own people. Week after week, as he begins the preparation of another sermon, he will write out in his notes the names or initials of a dozen or more of the people with whom he has had pastoral dealings in recent days, together with the temptation, problem, doubt, grief, or other need which brings each to mind.[14] From that time on, his study of the text will also be a study of and with these people. They will raise their own questions in his mind concerning the text, as he sees it increasingly through their eyes. The text, in turn, will put them in question, search their motives, interrogate them concerning the adequacy of what they are asking of life. Into his notebook will go a dialogue between the text and his people from which will rise germinal insight for the sermon.

In examining his own experience he will press this mutual interpretation to still more personal levels. "Have *I* really

---

[13] I have discussed this approach to preaching at length in chapter 4 of my book *Preaching to the Contemporary Mind* (Nashville: Abingdon Press, 1963).

[14] *Ibid.*, pp. 20-21.

heard and heeded what the Word is saying here?" he will ask himself. "How have I obeyed it? How faithfully? At what cost? What difference has it made in my life? How have I been sinning against it? What has my blindness or disobedience cost me? How has it hurt others?" This confessional, too, will go into his notebook, providing further access to the subject matter of the text. For every real text of the Scriptures arose out of just such searching encounter with living men; when the encounter is renewed, one best sees the serious purpose of the passage. As the text puts the interpreter himself in question, throwing light on the meaning of his life, it best speaks its own deep intent.

From such interplay of text and experience have come the great hours of the pulpit. Phillips Brooks spoke forcefully of "two aspects of the minister's work, which we are constantly meeting in the New Testament"—"message" and "witness."

"This is the message which we have heard of Him and declare unto you," says St. John in his first Epistle. "We are His witnesses of these things," says St. Peter before the Council at Jerusalem. In these two words together . . . we have the fundamental conception of the matter of all Christian preaching. It is to be a message given to us for transmission, but yet a message which we cannot transmit until it has entered into our own experience, and we can give our own testimony of its spiritual power. . . . If you and I can always carry this double consciousness, that we are messengers, and that we are witnesses, we shall have in our preaching all the authority and independence of assured truth, and yet all the appeal and convincingness of personal belief.[15]

[15] *On Preaching* (Paperback ed.; New York: The Seabury Press, 1964), pp. 14-15.

His understanding of this interpretative interaction left its imprint on the sermons through which Brooks still speaks. In a Palm Sunday sermon, taking as its text Mark 11:9, there is carefully detailed attention to the total passage, yet from beginning to end Brooks was talking not so much about the text as about us. After an initial paragraph in which he visualized the procession among the palms, he said:

What I want to do . . . is to see how . . . the soul of each of us is represented by Jerusalem, and how His Palm Sunday offer of Himself to His own city is repeated in the offer which Christ makes of Himself to every heart. . . . He comes to one of us as He came to that city of His Father's. . . . There was His Father's temple. There was the whole machinery for making the complete manhood. And yet there was defiance, selfishness, unspirituality, and cruelty—the house of prayer turned into the den of thieves. . . . I want to speak not so much of what is in His soul as of what is in the soul to which He comes. It cannot be indifferent to Him. And there does not come out one clear, simple utterance of reception or rejection, any more than Jerusalem was unanimous and prompt to receive or reject the Saviour when he came to her. From the soul, as from the city, come various answers, uttering the various portions of its complex life.[16]

After setting his direction in an introduction which thus strongly stated his purpose to interpret us in the light of the text, Brooks developed the sermon in a fourfold pattern.

"And first," he said, "there is in every soul something that spontaneously welcomes Christ." In a swift section he called forth the responsiveness of men, which resembles the "children and the common people" who welcomed Christ on

[16] *Sermons for the Principal Festivals and Fasts of the Church Year,* (New York: E. P. Dutton and Company, 1910), pp. 210-12.

the first Palm Sunday. "But now," he continued, "turn to some other parts in us and see how they receive Him, see how they correspond to other elements which were there in the streets of Jerusalem on that Palm Sunday."

He talked then of the skeptical Sadducees, letting them hold the mirror to "the skeptic in us poisoning the faith of the believer in us." In a third section he passed beyond those who doubted Christ to those who hated him. But after a few words about the Pharisees, this section also turned to us.

If there is in your heart at this moment any hard, proud, selfish, narrow notion of religion which you would have to see cast down and trodden underfoot before the breadth and the humility of the Gospel faith could take entire possession of your soul, then, tell me, have you not within you an element which corresponds exactly to what the Pharisees were in Jerusalem? And if you are living in sins of any sort which are deliberate and obstinate, which you do not mean to give up, and which Christ hates, with which he cannot live, then there is that in you which hates Christ.[17]

Having developed this assertion, he moved to a final section in which he spoke briefly of the Roman soldiers—cold, contemptuous foreigners, power-conscious and earthy, wholly out of touch with the meaning of the event they policed. "What better picture could you have of that which so many men know only too well as a true element of their internal life?" he asked.

Hard earthly prudence; a coarse terrestrial corner of our nature, to which all spiritual truths seem to make their appeal in vain; an iron unsusceptibility to all enthusiasm; a disposition to or-

_____
[17] *Ibid.*, p. 217.

24

ganize life upon its lower plane, and to think of religious impulses and aspirations only as the disturbers of the peace; materialism; selfishness; reason boasting itself of its confinement to its most terrestrial activities; the tyranny of sense—oh, what an element that is in all of us! [18]

After painting this picture with almost unbearable realism, Brooks concluded with an invitation to receive Christ's forgiveness and live. "The moment that you trust Christ's forgiveness, and in profound gratitude give yourself to His service, casting every reluctance and doubt aside, that moment He begins the purification and salvation of your life which shall go on throughout eternity. May some one, may many of you, do that today." [19]

Thus vividly have the master preachers brought text, pastoral understanding of their people, and relentless searching of their own hearts into conversation with one another. Use of the text as interpreter of our life gives Brooks's sermon its freshness of appeal across an intervening century.

In this searching of contemporary life and his own soul, the minister finds the safeguard against the drabness and inauthenticity which easily engulf us. "Hearsay has swallowed up the world," wrote Hugo von Hoffmansthal.[20] It threatens to swallow up the pulpit. We repeat at secondhand what we have read in commentaries, illustrate with swift gleanings from here and there, and leave over it all a sense of remoteness and unreality. Not only does it rob our preaching of the

[18] *Ibid.*, p. 219.

[19] *Ibid.*, p. 221.

[20] Quoted by Helmut Thielicke in *The Trouble with the Church* (New York: Harper & Row, 1965), p. 45.

urgency and interest which belong to the gospel; it leaves men wondering if what we say is not a performance given because it is required of us when the church bells ring, making the preacher one more paid propagandist in a world of hired voices. If the gospel is to carry conviction in such a world, the preacher, above all others, needs to speak with what Von Hoffmansthal called "his own peculiar tone." This he can do when his weekly preparation brings a fresh meeting of text, parish life, and personal self-examination in their own fresh encounter within his mind and heart.

MAKING PREACHING PRESENT TENSE

The aim of the sermon, Gerhard Ebeling declares, is to let "the text become God's Word again." [21] It is not the *text* which is to be proclaimed, but God's Word, understood as an encounter between God and the listener, which *involves* the text but is *more* than the text. In a useful metaphor John Knox points out that true preaching must always be one elliptical reality drawn around two foci, one in the world and one in the text. And this, he says is not so much for reasons of psychological interest as for theological validity, since the text was first spoken to a human situation and cannot be understood unless it is approached through a like situation in which we are existentially involved.[22] James T. Cleland takes up the figure and draws it into a diagram in which the good news and the contemporary situation are the foci and the enclosing ellipse is labeled, not "the sermon," but "the Word of God." To underscore what the diagram makes clear,

[21] *Word and Faith*, p. 329.
[22] Cf. *The Integrity of Preaching* (Nashville: Abingdon Press, 1957), p. 22.

26

he declares explicitly that "a Word of God is always the Good News (or an aspect of it) immersed in a Contemporary Situation." [23]

Within the New Testament the one *kerygma* is proclaimed in common by all the books, yet each book presents it in its own characteristic way as the good news confronts a different situation, so that the Word emerges in the meeting of the unchanging message and the new human need. This fresh encounter with varied situations gives the several books their vivid individuality despite the fact that they are all concerned with the same good news.

The text deals with "past occurrence of the Word of God." As such it comprises an indispensable and vastly important record. But its function is not to be studied as past record so much as to provide the occasion for a present Word to these men now confronted. "Its aim," as Ebeling writes, "is, that there should be further proclamation. . . . Proclamation that has taken place is to become proclamation that takes place." And, he adds, this "does not normally happen through recitation." [24] It happens rather through direct address to the present hearer, showing him his own life in the light of the text. "The sermon begins by announcing that John in prison was bewildered, and so are we; it continues by pointing out that he took his trouble directly to Jesus, and so must we; and comes to its climax by reminding us that he got only an indirect answer, and so do we." [25]

Gerhard Ebeling makes a helpful distinction between *ex-*

[23] *Preaching to Be Understood* (Nashville: Abingdon Press, 1965), p. 44.

[24] *Word and Faith*, p. 329.

[25] Paul Scherer, *The Word God Sent* (New York: Harper & Row, 1965), p. 77.

position and *execution* of the text. "The sermon as such is in point of fact not *exposition* of the text—whereby exposition here means the concentration on the historical task of understanding. For to understand this text as a text means to understand it in its historical givenness as proclamation that has taken place." This, of course, is a basic workshop step which the preacher must take and on which he dares spare no pains in discovering the original meaning and intent. "But the sermon as a sermon is not exposition of the text as past proclamation, but is itself proclamation in the present—and that means, then, that *the sermon is* EXECUTION *of the text*. It carries into execution the aim of the text. It is proclamation of what the text has proclaimed." [26]

It may not be inappropriate to test our preaching by the prevailing tenses of its verbs. If there are too many past and perfect tenses, do they not point to "past occurrence of the Word of God," "proclamation that has taken place," smothering the urgency of present proclamation? We are not called principally to recount the past, but to discover and declare its truth in terms of present possibilities. John Dillenberger calls attention to the changing theories of atonement as instances of the repeated reconfrontation of the one past event on Calvary with the emerging needs of successive generations.

The notion of redemption from cosmic powers and forces of evil expressed the ancient world's way of understanding redemption as the direct, personal release from such powers; the theory of satisfaction had to do with social structures in which relations of lords and serfs in large part played their role; the so-called moral influence theory of the atonement was developed

[26] *Word and Faith,* pp. 330 f.

in a social context in which to be incorporated into the actuality of love made manifest seemed a realizable teleological direction. It is not by accident that in our own day we experience redemption as deliverance from meaninglessness, anxiety, despair, loneliness, frustration, etc.[27]

What the honored theologians whose names are linked with these atonement theories have done for the men of their times, the preacher is called to do in the midst of the thronging events he shares with his people.

In Exodus 33:17-23, on the one hand, and the mid-twentieth-century proclamation that "God is dead," on the other, a difficult scripture and a trying contemporary issue can meet in creative confrontation. To study the passage as historic event and seek thereafter to make modern applications can leave the listener with a sense of unreality in which no present Word from the Lord reaches him. To deal with the "God is dead" issue topically, from whatever may be the minister's peculiar orientation on the theological map, may produce an informative essay but is not likely to carry the authentic note of the gospel. But the text may be allowed to speak directly to the need created by the emerging issue in a way that brings authentic gospel into living experience.

"You cannot see my face; for man shall not see me and live" (Exod. 33:20), the preacher reads, adding immediately: "We turn that around. God shall not see modern man and live, we say." Quickly he sketches the issue with which

[27] "On Broadening the New Hermeneutic," in *The New Hermeneutic*, p. 161. The aspects of atonement enumerated here have not merely historic connotations, but may speak with peculiar relevance to the varied needs of individuals today, as I have tried to show in *Living Doctrine in a Vital Pulpit* (Nashville: Abingdon Press, 1964), pp. 156-65.

29

we are confronted. This ancient story, he says, speaks a word of clarity into our confusion. We cannot dismiss it as mere primitive anthropomorphism. In these symbolic images we become witnesses to a profound encounter in which Moses, a pivotal character in whom history turned a crucial corner, grew into one of his most mature and creative insights. Even more, this is *our* encounter. See what it says to *us*.

It declares that God is indeed dead, if his name means what we have often made it stand for. Like Moses, saying "Show me thy glory" (vs. 18)—asking a full disclosure of God because he needed the strength this knowledge would give him in the business of making a nation of a band of slaves—we have wanted to know God in order to use him. We argue that religion is a good thing because it will stabilize society, strengthen democracy, build a rampart against communism, promote success, guarantee our peace of mind. The Harris survey has reported that 97 percent of our people believe in God, though more than half of us hardly ever feel concern about the pollution of our rivers, or the rigidity with which we limit immigration, or the treatment we have accorded many Jews. More than a third of us are seldom concerned about our food surplus in the presence of terrible hunger, or the fact that some people still live in slums, or the way Negroes are treated in the United States. To believe in God but remain unconcerned about these things is to seek a god tailored to our uses. God the Creator cares about the creation we pollute. God the Redeemer loves the world we neglect. God the Father of our Lord Jesus Christ carries the lost and forgotten in his heart. The God who can sanction our unconcern is dead indeed. He never really lived.

But the death of this God, the preacher may continue,

opens the way to a vital encounter with the God of all reality. He says to us, as to Moses, "I will proclaim before you my name 'The Lord' " (vs. 19). As Lord, he is not our intimate, to be set down with defining finality in our creeds, nor the object of our investigation, nor a conclusion drawn from our logical proofs. Yet we can know him through what he does, what happens in decisive experiences to which we are party. He still says, "I will make all my goodness pass before you" (vs. 19) and comes to us through mighty acts, remembered from the Scriptures and encountered in events that change our lives. He is not at our disposal; we meet him on *his* terms, as he says: "I will be gracious to whom I will be gracious, and will show mercy on whom I will show mercy" (vs. 19). We can meet him only in obedient, dependent faith. Though any lesser god is indeed dead, this God of demanding but gracious reality is very much alive.

And while we cannot have him at our disposal, the preacher concludes, he shows us all we need to know of him. To us, as to Moses, God says: "You shall see my back; but my face shall not be seen" (vs. 23). Like us, Moses had been called by the stern voice of conscience to difficult tasks which seemed too big for him. His people's slavery had commandeered his conscience, even though he himself had escaped. Under God, he felt, their liberation demanded something of him. The burden of their need—and their irresponsibility in the midst of it—rested heavily on his shoulders, even as it must on ours when human rights are denied. God's call is always a call to struggle against whatever oppresses his children. To hear his call is to be involved.

This pictorial scene portrays Moses as hidden in the cleft of a rock (vs. 22) while God passed by. For us who can sing,

31

> Rock of Ages, cleft for me,
>   Let me hide myself in thee;
> Let the water and the blood,
>   From thy wounded side which flowed,
> Be of sin the double cure,
>   Save from wrath and make me pure,

that Rock where we meet God is the person of Jesus Christ. In him we meet the gracious acts that make life new. From him we receive the calls that claim our conscience in the issues of our time. Finding in him one whom we can call nothing less than Savior and Lord, we know a living God.

In such encounter of past proclamation and present issue we see the characteristic that makes the Bible the medium of God's Word to all men: It finds us where we are. This, then, is the characteristic of the text for which the preacher must make persistent, passionate search. "What does it say to *my people now?*" he asks. *To get hold of a text by the handle that makes it the medium for valid preaching is to search out the aspect of it which interprets our life, mirrors our minds and judges them, shows us who we are in our lostness and our possibilities.* Historical reconstruction will not do this, though it may help the preacher's workshop thinking by bringing out the truth in which we are mirrored. When, beyond historical inquiry, textual study discovers how "in dealings with the text *its* being interpreted by us turns into *our* being interpreted by the text," [28] we have the material for preaching in which men encounter a Word of God to them.

Discussion of men's problems, exploration of their quan-

[28] See note 11, p. 20.

daries, attempts to answer their insistent questions, cannot be counted on to produce such preaching. The problem may be graphic and gripping, but a mere topical discussion of its urgencies is in danger of missing the authentic note of the gospel. The preacher's wisdom is not sufficient for such grapplings, nor are men in church for one more exposure to human wisdom. It is when "the text by means of the sermon becomes a hermeneutic aid in the understanding of present experience" that the issue of the hour is illumined by the searching light of the gospel.

In every congregation those are present who face such needs as were dramatized on the brink of a shell crater following the bombing of Stuttgart. Meeting Helmut Thielicke there, a woman said: "My husband died down there. His place was right under the hole. The clean-up squad was unable to find a trace of him; all that was left was his cap. We were there the last time you preached in the cathedral church. And here before this pit I want to thank you for preparing him for eternity." [29] Preaching is called to this task as, week by week, eternity confronts men and women in the temptations, decisions, pressing issues, decisive events which fill their days. When the interpreter can so bring text and experience together as to reveal the meaning of their lives, they may hear a Word from the Lord and respond.

Is it presumptuous to suppose that preaching can thus partake of the nature of revelation? In what sense is it true that the text becomes God's Word? What does this mean for the work of the preacher? To these questions the next chapter must give attention.

[29] Helmut Thielicke, *Our Heavenly Father* (New York: Harper & Row, 1960), pp. 65-66.

For Further Study

What a short chapter on a big subject can do is strictly limited. It can draw a circle around a problem and point a direction, but what happens then depends on the reader. If he is a serious student of the interperter's task, he will pursue the idea back to its roots and on to its consequences. To help him do that, I suggest that we follow each of these chapters with a little informal conference. The reader, of course, has the option of coming or staying away!

In these after-the-chapter chats we can talk about some books and suggest some useful projects. We shall not even pretend that the books suggested comprise a complete bibliography. Rather we shall point to a few, selected for their peculiar vitality in putting depth under the chapter's idea and giving wings to its implications. The projects will be a few things the serious reader can do, in living and working with the Interpreting Word, to begin immediately to let its power into his preaching. Some will lead to long-range practices, others to sharpening up that next sermon.

Many of the best benefits of our hours together will come *after* you have read the chapter and left the "conference." Pursuing the idea for yourself with other reading, you will add stature to your own thinking. Chapter idea plus broader slants from other directions plus your own thinking will equal sharper insight—perhaps greater wisdom! The voices in the books will not be a chorus of agreement. Sometimes you will have to moderate their debate; if you stay with it, you will come away with a tougher mind and some convictions that will stand by you. The projects will sharpen your skill as an interpreter of the Word that interprets *us*.

1. For the deeper roots of this chapter idea—and as background for much that follows—two rather difficult books will greatly reward the reader who will pay the price of some hard study. They are *The New Hermeneutic,* edited by James M. Robinson and John B. Cobb, Jr. (New York: Harper & Row, 1964) and *Word and Faith,* by Gerhard Ebeling (Philadelphia: Fortress Press, 1963). The first contains two important and vigorously suggestive papers by Ebeling and Ernst Fuchs, which are then discussed from varied viewpoints by a group of American scholars. The second offers a series of theological essays in which Ebeling grapples with many aspects of the Word and the interpreter's task.

2. Having suggested two difficult background books, let us turn to some delightful reading to speed you on your way. *The Trouble with the Church,* by Helmut Thielicke (New York: Harper & Row, 1965) is an inspiring discussion of preaching by one of the greatest preachers of this century. *Preaching to Be Understood,* by James T. Cleland (Nashville: Abingdon Press, 1965), contains the ripe wisdom of one of the strongest teachers of preaching. Both discuss aspects of the matter treated in this chapter—and much more! You will have noted that this chapter does not altogether agree with Karl Barth's *The Preaching of the Gospel* (Philadelphia: The Westminster Press, 1963), but why not see for yourself? It is a small book by the giant theologian. Whether you fully subscribe to its position or not, you will find it rewarding in its content and charming in its manner.

3. One of the "long-range practices" you might begin to employ is suggested on pages 20 and 21. You may well begin the habit of writing down on a worksheet, as you begin to prepare a sermon, such a list of persons and the needs you

have observed in your contact with them. Of course, you will guard confidences! Without describing individuals, you can bring your text into dialogue with these needs. You'll be surprised how much more you'll find in the text.

On the same worksheet write your self-examination before the text. Whether any of this goes into the sermon or not, you'll preach with greater vividness and urgency.

4. Now for the immediate. Suppose you tackle a sermon with the conscious attempt to make your work with the text not so much *exposition* as *execution*. There are a couple of nucleus ideas in this chapter, which you could develop—or take one which has grown out of your own Bible reading. You might approach Luke 7:18-23 in the way quoted on page 27. Or the interchange with Exodus 33:17-23 found on pages 29-32 is considerably short of being a sermon; you might make it your own by your fresh study of the passage and the current problem, and then preach *your* sermon on it.

5. If you'd like to see how one of the most virile biblical preachers now at work goes about this business of *execution* of the text, pay close attention to the sermons of Paul Scherer. I suggest an analytical reading of "Take That Thine Is," in his *The Word God Sent* (New York: Harper & Row, 1965). Note how, in such a sermon, Scherer is constantly putting the text to work and just as steadily talking about *us*. Note how immediately the process starts in the opening lines of the sermon. Then go through it, paragraph by paragraph, and note the myriad ways in which this text and our life speak to each other. Does it suggest some ways in which you could keep such vital dialogue going when you interpret the Word?

2

The Text Becomes God's Word

TODAY'S CRISIS IN PREACHING

Answers to a recent questionnaire reflect nothing less than a major crisis in preaching. "The Protestant pulpit," wrote one churchgoer, "is held in low esteem in the minds of many of my acquaintances." In similar vein another said: "Most of my friends consider the Protestant pulpit to be irrelevant, fearful, and not very scholarly; many in our parish regard the pulpit as harmless and boring." Still another spoke of "bland sermons with obvious 'quotes' which they have just picked up somewhere and which do not really come out of their own reading, studying, or personal experience—what I call 'canned homiletics.' " [1] Thus do listeners limn the features of a pulpit which has lost any basis of authority held in common by preacher and congregation.

Its word is not heard in the context of a church which believes in verbal inspiration. The *words* of its texts are no longer understood as authentic words of God. Since God does not convey his truth in propositions, texts are not eternal pronouncements needing only to be explained and applied. Having lost this note of direct authority as the chief interpreter of an infallible Bible, and having failed to enter into full possession of any adequate alternative understanding of the authority of the Word, the pulpit has been left hesitant and stammering. But a grasp of what it means that *the text interprets us* can help it recover its lost power.

In psychotherapy, when a patient sees the meaning of events that once disrupted his life—enters into insights that have become his own inner history freshly relived, not the echo of something told him by another—that moment of revelation can change his life. And when the vital events of the Scriptures are appropriated as the story of our life, they speak with the authority of inner immediacy.

A too common failure to interpret the Scriptures in the light of this inner authority has contributed to an alarming lapse of significant knowledge of the Bible. A wide-ranging survey documents this loss with abundant specifics. It finds, for instance, that "More than half the Presbyterian and Congregational members" of churches in the sample county "had no knowledge of the Old Testament prophets." The

---

[1] Donald Macleod, "The Middle Atlantic Pulpit," in *The Pulpit*, XXXV (September, 1964), 11.

paucity of information was even deeper, the report added, among Methodists, United Lutherans, Augustana Lutherans, and Disciples.[2] Fewer than one third of the Methodists, Congregationalists, and United Lutherans studied could "find in the good Samaritan parable an admonition to provide aid to others, or, to express it another way, . . . more than a third of their people had no idea of any meaning that might be attached to this parable." [3] As the survey moved from one communion to another, it reported that the various denominations presented similar degrees of "unfamiliarity with the Biblical foundations and their relevance for the contemporary scene." [4]

In Protestantism, with its stress on the centrality of the sermon in worship, there is maximum opportunity to help men rediscover the authority and relevance of the Scriptures as interpreting their life. In the emergence of successive generations for whom this has not been done, the crisis of the pulpit casts a long shadow before it—the crisis of a biblically starved church and a society whose conscience is no longer nurtured in biblical insight.

Lacking a sense of commanding reality in the Bible as giving meaning and directive to their life, men draw their formative insights and compelling motives from contemporary culture. Even within the church they seek conformity not to biblical teaching but to the patterns of society. An organized body of Methodist ministers and laymen typified this trend when they sent to the resident bishop of their area a

[2] Victor Obenhaus, *The Church and Faith in Mid-America* (Philadelphia: The Westminster Press, 1963), p. 77.
[3] *Ibid.*, p. 79.
[4] *Ibid.*, p. 155.

petition signed by an impressively long list of persons, demanding the denomination's withdrawal from the National Council of Churches because, they alleged, it was "agitating the race problem"; denouncing the use of church publications "to agitate the race problem"; and calling for a halt in efforts to integrate local churches and abolish the all-Negro Central Jurisdiction. In his resolute reply the bishop could speak meaningfully only in biblical terms: "The Methodist Church is a part of the body of Christ. Its witness to the love and saving grace of our Lord and Savior Jesus Christ will continue despite the disagreement among its members over these issues." [5] To the churchmen gripped by the standards of their community this biblical language can speak with convincing authority only if they have entered into it by personal appropriation which makes it the interpreter of their own life and times. A pulpit which has failed to open avenues of interpretation to this end has failed to fulfill its main calling.

In this crisis of the pulpit a return to preaching which opens the Scriptures as our own inner history is mandatory. Paul shows its movement in I Corinthians 1:17-25, as he reviews his own proclamation. It was preaching through event, not argument, he said: "not with eloquent wisdom, lest the cross of Christ be emptied of its power" (vs. 17). The Cross confronted his listeners as a towering event, in the light of which they saw the meaning of their lives. Words, propositions, "eloquent wisdom" must be secondary to that. But the objective *happenedness* of the Cross was of small effect until a subjective appropriation had been made. "The word

[5] Bishop Edward J. Pendergrass as reported in the *First Church Review*, First Methodist Church, Evanston, Illinois, September 18, 1965.
40

of the cross is folly to those who are perishing"—who regard it casually or critically as outside observers. "But to us who are being saved"—who have entered into its meaning until it has become our own—"it is the power of God" (vs. 18). Revelation comes *through* history, but it becomes operative when it so engages our firsthand experience as to interpret us to ourselves.

GROUND PLAN OF OUR LIFE

To say that the text comes alive when our interpretation of it turns into *its* interpertation of *us* is not to rob it of its own objective authority. The text does more than read out of *us* what is in us. It contributes to the understanding of our life as oriented by events and insights which have an unyielding objectivity. The Word searches us, judges us, saves us; and it saves only as it searches and judges.

In common usage "word" is a confusing symbol. We know it as the basic unit of language, something spoken, written, communicated. How, then, is the Bible God's Word? Not as his *words*. Within the biblical documents "word" is often more like an act than an utterance. "And God said, 'Let there be light'; and there was light." (Gen. 1:3.) This word-event bond is the recurring theme of the creation story: "And God said, . . . and it was so." When the insight emerges "that man does not live by bread alone, but that man lives by everything that proceeds out of the mouth of the Lord" (Deut. 8:3), its background is not something *spoken* but something *done* in the events of the Exodus. God's attempt to make his Word known proceeds not so much through extended speech as through the unfolding drama of the Bible. When it reaches its climax in Jesus, John declares

41

that "the Word became flesh and dwelt among us" (1:14).

Even beyond Jesus as historic person, this utterance through event advances in the Christ-event prolonged in the church, as the Letter to the Colossians declares: the apostolic office was given "to make the word of God fully known, the mystery hidden for ages and generations but now made manifest to his saints" (1:25-26). As chapter 1 has shown, there is a sense in which the Word of God to us is the ellipse drawn around the two foci of the "good news" as it comes to us in a biblical text and the emergent situation of need or decision in which we stand. To the question, Is the Bible the Word of God? we can reply with Karl Barth: "A more precise statement of the truth would be to say that the Bible *becomes* God's Word, and when it becomes this for us, then it is so." [6]

With peculiar aptness, Gerhard Ebeling speaks of the Word as having *happened.* "The word that once happened and in happening became the text must again become word with the help of the text and thus happen as interpreting word." [7] In such interpretation preaching participates in revelation. Through the insight that emerges from this fresh dialogue of text with situation God precipitates his encounter with men.

Where this occurs the pulpit is still vibrant with saving power. Any close reading of the sermons of such a vital preacher as Helmut Thielicke makes clear that his capacity to lay bare the power of the Bible to interpret us underlies his life-changing effectiveness. In the introduction to one of his memorable sermons he makes this use of the text explicit. Describing his infant son's delighted recognition of

---

[6] *The Preaching of the Gospel*, p. 46.
[7] *The New Hermeneutic*, p. 68.

the baby in the mirror as himself, he adds that this is what happens in our most valid reading of the biblical events:

Suddenly *our* face may change too, and we are compelled to say, "There I am, actually. This is I." All of a sudden we have identified the hero of this tale and now we can read the whole story in the first person. Truly this is no small thrill. This is the way we must move back and forth until we have identified ourselves with the many people who surrounded Jesus. For as long as we fail to recognize *ourselves* in these people we fail to recognize our *Lord*.[8]

That is, if this is only a story about *these people,* and not about us, Jesus may be *their* Lord, but he is not recognized as ours. So, Thielicke continues,

the best thing to do is always to take up your position at exactly the same spot where one of the persons who meet him or appear in his parables stands; to stand, for example, where John is in prison, addressing doubting questions to him, or the Canaanite woman, who desires nothing of him but the crumbs that fall from the Lord's table, or the rich young ruler, who will not forsake the god Mammon and so goes away unblessed.[9]

When we enter into the biblical scenes by this direct appropriation, they speak to us with compelling authority. For, as Thielicke observes, "In every one of these stories we find sketched out the ground plan of our own life." [10] With first-

[8] *The Waiting Father,* by Helmut Thielicke (New York: Harper & Row, 1959), p. 18.
[9] *Ibid.*
[10] *Ibid.*

hand clarity and conviction we see ourselves and the way we must go. The struggle which fills the Bible from beginning to end becomes our struggle. The reign of God and the kingdom of evil cease to be concepts about which we can discourse and speculate as dispassionate observers; in their warfare our life is at stake. The symbolism of the struggle shows itself as "the ground plan of our own life." We see in Israel's Egyptian bondage our slavery to sin, in the Exodus our liberation. The enemies of Israel, especially as they appear in the poetry of the psalms, become the sins and evils that lay waste our life. Israel's turning to false defenders holds the mirror to the failing defenses that have betrayed us.

> They have ears, but do not hear;
>   noses, but do not smell.
> They have hands, but do not feel;
>   feet, but do not walk;
>   and they do not make a sound in their throat.
> Those who make them are like them;
>   so are all who trust in them.
>
> O Israel, trust in the Lord!
>   He is their help and their shield.
> O house of Aaron, put your trust in the Lord!
>   He is their help and their shield.
> You who fear the Lord, trust in the Lord!
>   He is their help and their shield.
>
> The Lord has been mindful of us; he will bless us;
>
> .   .   .   .
>
> he will bless those who fear the Lord,
>   both small and great. (Ps. 115:6-13.)

That becomes our personal cry, the echo of our past, the conviction of our present, the hope of our future. In the New Testament the victory of Christ's death and resurrection has been won *for us,* though we must hold out to the end to claim our part in it. Our Lord is speaking to us of our struggles as he says: "But take heed to yourselves; for they will deliver you up to councils; and you will be beaten in synagogues; and you will stand before governors and kings for my sake, to bear testimony before them" (Mark 13:9). Temptations, sufferings, trials are not indifferent circumstance, nor evils to which escape is the only relevant answer; they are our life in the world, through which we are called to make our witness. In the midst of them we recognize our Lord's personal assurance that "he who endures to the end will be saved" (Mark 13:13). The struggle is our struggle; the victory is for us. When the text interprets us, we hear in it God's Word.

REVELATION THROUGH INNER HISTORY

Revelation inheres in the biblical history *received as our history.* That insight can nurture restored vitality amid the perils to today's crisis in preaching. Revelation does not inhabit a set of documents. It is not words in a book, nor is it an idea crossing the mind. It *reveals* when it so grips one of God's children as to illumine his self-understanding, show him what his life is about, arrest him on his way and redirect his course. When this occurs, he knows that he has met reality from beyond himself, that God has revealed himself in the meeting.

The power of external event to become our own inner history finds some faint shadow in the scene enacted daily at the Lincoln Memorial in Washington. In steady procession, men, women, and children from many national and racial strains enter the shrine, linger for a time, and leave, often visibly moved by what they have met. Not only does the benign presence portrayed by the sculptor grip them; they often pause to read at least snatches of the two supreme Lincoln addresses carved on the walls which flank the statue. "Fourscore and seven years ago, our fathers brought forth, upon this continent, a new nation." *Our* fathers? But these people come from southern Europe, the Far East, Africa, the islands of the seas. Not in any external sense are the fathers of whom Lincoln wrote *their* fathers. Yet it is precisely in their growing ability to say "our fathers" and mean by it Lincoln and those to whom he applied the term, that this motley company learns what America means. As the external events become their own inner history, they are recipients of a revelation, not only about the land of their adoption but about the meaning of their life in it.[11]

In a sense more profoundly structural to our life we enter into the biblical history as intimately our own, and, in this internalization of its persons and events, receive God's revelation of himself and of the new life in him. The biblical language is a language of action, not of generalized laws and principles, lending itself to our need to understand in relation to vivid images. Adam and Eve, facing the disruption of their being, are not two ancients but our mirror images. The men of Babel, desperately reaching for an earth-based heaven and thrown into chaotic misunderstanding of one another, show us ourselves with our pretentions and be-

[11] Cf. *The Meaning of Revelation,* by H. Richard Niebuhr (New York: The Macmillan Company, 1941).

wildering disaffections. Abraham, drawn into covenant by
the grace of God, is not merely the father of the people
Israel, but our father. Bondage in Egypt and liberation in
the Exodus light up great areas of our experinece. In the
darkness of the Exile and the new springtime of the restoration we understand much that God does for us in life's sterner
passages. The voices of the prophets, lifted in these formative
hours of the world's history, become for us—far more than
echoes of a remote yesterday—springs of insight in which
we grasp the meaning of today.

The possessive pronouns of the Bible are pointers to this
meaning. Hear Paul say "my." "I thank my God," he writes
to the Romans (1:8); "I thank my God," to the Philippians
(1:3); "I thank my God," to Philemon (vs. 4). Nothing
could be farther from Paul's mind than any notion of possessive claim on God. Not in this sense does he say "my," but
to denote the committed bond by which he has entered into
the life shared in God through our Lord Jesus Christ. "According to my gospel," he writes, repeating the phrase twice
over in the Letter to the Romans (2:16 and 16:25); yet he
would be the first to deny any claim that the gospel belonged
to him! Far from possessive, he spent his days in the dangerous, fierce excitement of giving it away. Writing "my gospel," he conveys the reality of the good news to which his
whole life is oriented, within whose vast horizons he finds its
glad meaning and indomitable purpose.

Listen to the precious and mysterious "thy" in God's address to us: "I am the Lord thy God" (Deut. 5:6 KJV).
That one word, said Luther, contains God's promise of himself to us, so that within it are wrapped all the great things
it is faith's business to receive. "In it," he marveled, "you will

find Christ, life, victory over death and the resurrection of the dead to life eternal, indeed the whole of the Old and New Testament." [12] For that one word holds the difference between cold, dry doctrine preserved in an ancient book, and all that fills life with significance, joy, and fulfillment.

For this appropriation of inner history our Lord's post-resurrection confrontation of Thomas is chiefly memorable. Until that moment, the Resurrection had been for Thomas an external event to which speculative questions—Did it happen? Could it happen? What evidence can you show that it happened?—were the most pertinent response. World shaking though the event might be, it could have little impact on *Thomas'* world while it remained thus an external event. In the encounter, however, something personal transpired, calling for response in personal appropriation, so that Thomas was left exclaiming, *"My* Lord and *my* God!" (John 20:28, italics added), and in that moment the whole understanding of his life was reshaped. "Have you believed because you have seen me?" asked Jesus. "Blessed are those who have not seen and yet believe" (John 20:29). For them the outer experience must be necessarily secondhand. Not granted the visual encounter of the first witnesses, they must begin with the external reports. But they need not remain at that beginning point. For they, no less than Thomas, may enter in and make the experience their own, the configuration of their lives remade as they too cry, *"My* Lord and *my* God!" When that experience is reached, in the twentieth century as in the first, it is necessarily firsthand.

Heinrich Ott speaks helpfully of this distinction in somewhat different language, drawing a contrast between the "successive" and the "structural" in our relation of ourselves to the biblical events.[13] What is "successive" is removed from immediate impact on my life by its remoteness in a time sequence, but what is "structural" provides a framework by which I understand myself and support my decisions. The speech habits of mere time sequence still linger in much of our preaching concerning the early chapters of Genesis, for example, even when we have come to a sophisticated understanding of theological myth as opposed to literal history. The preacher often speaks of Adam as if he were an individual man living at a datable time. Such preaching falls on the modern ear with the hollow ring of unreality. This language of time sequence plunges us into the absurdities of vain attempts to harmonize garden-of-Eden poetry with twentieth-century cosmology. Despite our best efforts, such handling leaves the experience in the realm of the external. Far different is the language which deals with these events as "structural," which sees that we do not live *since* Adam so much as *in* Adam, or perhaps *as* Adam. The preacher who would help men of today hear the early chapters of Genesis as a Word of God to them, cannot say too plainly of such an event, "This is not a once-upon-a-time story, but an always-and-everywhere story. This is not the story of one man, but of every man. It is your story and mine."

We shall need to be at pains to discover images which lift the material out of the thought forms of time sequence into those more structural to our self-understanding. Adam and Eve, plunged into the vast disruption of their spoiled

[13] Cf. *Theology and Preaching* (Philadelphia: The Westminster Press, 1965), pp. 86-87.

Eden, are visual symbols of our broken life. Lorado Taft's sculpture, "The Solitude of the Soul," one of the treasures of the Art Institute of Chicago, may well pose the question whether the artist is portraying them, or us, or us in them. Men and women carved from separate faces of one great marble, only partially able to see one another, strain to reach around the dividing corners to make contact in an association that is more nearly separation. Is this our life, as we share our broken Eden?

So deep is our disruption that the Chicago Police Department has written it into a book for parents to use in making their children wary of strangers who might molest them. Done with good children's book technique, it shows one picture to a page, with a few accompanying words of text. Beneath a hulking, fearsome figure, one reads, "This is Mr. Stranger." Successive drawings develop the character, with unfolding text which says: "He can be called Mr. Danger. . . . Let us call him Mr. Stranger-Danger. . . . Mr. Stranger-Danger is like a strange dog. . . . He is not your friend, and he will hurt you." Such is the tragic brokenness of our life that in the mythologies which shape our children's minds we feel forced to weld the bond of rhyme and lurid picture between "stranger" and "danger." Desperately we need to learn that every man is our brother, yet such are the actualities of Metropolis that children must know too the hazards of Mr. Stranger-Danger.

Implementing, with such valid images as we can find, the structural nature of the material with which we deal, we can help men enter into it as illuminating who they are and where they stand. Adam's broken Eden is ours; men must see that if they are to see in the story anything that matters. When

they have seen that, we can lead them into an equally structural understanding of the pride, presumption, and rebellion
which in us, as in Adam, shatter Eden and make the encounter with God not a promise but a fearfulness from which
we hide. That done, we may even lead them into some personal appropriation of the faith which finds in Jesus the hope
of mankind's broken home, and can say of him, "he is our
peace, who has made us both one, and has broken down
the dividing wall of hostility, . . . bringing the hostility to an
end" (Eph. 2:14, 16).

REACHING "MAN AS CONSCIENCE"

To enable men so to enter into the biblical events as the
story of their lives that the text becomes God's Word to
them, preaching takes as its principle of interpretation "man
as conscience." [14] When the text is so brought into contact
with our experience that it illuminates the meaning of who
we are and what we have been doing, the elements of response are already present—as they were when Nathan, having evoked David's indignation by the parable of the ewe
lamb, brought the matter home with his swift thrust: "You
are the man" (II Sam. 12:7). As Ernst Fuchs picturesquely
says, "At home one does not speak so that people may understand, but because people understand!" [15] To be sure, some
conversation at home is meant to convey information: "Time
to leave for school!" "The light bill is due." "There's a
chance of a promotion, but we can't be sure yet." But the
characteristic which most makes home talk precious is that

---

[14] Ebeling, *Word and Faith*, p. 332.
[15] "The New Testament and the Hermeneutical Problem" in *The New
Hermeneutic*, p. 124.

here we can say what is in our heart, for no other reason than that we need to say it and be understood. We do not speak so that people may understand, but because they understand. Is this not characteristic also of God's Word to us? There is that in conscience which understands, and we speak because conscience is listening.

"Words produce understanding only by appealing to experience and leading to experience," Ebeling reminds us. "Only where word has already taken place can word take place. Only where there is already previous understanding can understanding take place. Only a man who is already concerned with the matter in question can be claimed for it." [16] But men *are* concerned in their consciences. The vehemence of their denials is the measure of the depth of their concern. Their insistence that thorny issues of the time are off limits is itself their testimony that they understand only too well what is being said. The Word never touches them so intimately, nor moves so directly into the realm of inner history, as when it speaks to "man as conscience."

The call to preach is a call to speak thus. This is the glory and the peril of the preaching office. For, though men *understand* the Word which comes home to conscience, it is understatement to say that they scarcely *welcome* it. And weak men that we are, we shrink from what we fear will erect barriers between us and men among whom we live, whose burdens and guilt we share, many of whom we dearly love. Wanting, as we say, to "make something of ourselves," we dread to speak the word which may detract from popular leadership. As one church member said about his minister in an aggravated situation, "He couldn't take a stand on

[16] *Word and Faith*, p. 320.

that subject in his preaching—you see, he hopes to be a bishop." [17] In reporting the comment, Langdon Gilkey remarked that unfortunately no criticism of the minister was implied. It was assumed that this was, of course, the way a prudent man would act. So the crisis of the pulpit becomes the crisis of the church; for in Protestantism, where the centrality of the sermon makes it the chief medium of communion with God, the infiltration of the assumption that the pulpit must soften the challenge to conscience cuts off access to God's Word.

In one of its most paralyzing complications this inhibition takes the form of a widespread belief that the "spiritual" has no direct relation to troubled issues moving toward decision in our common life. An editorial in a news magazine of national importance gives vigorous expression to this separation. "Can members of a congregation feel as friendly or as receptive to a pastor's guidance after they have heard him express views contrary to their own conscientious beliefs?" it asks, and goes on to declare: "If the sermons were confined solely to spiritual matters, the layman would accept the interpretation given him as an expression of conscience. But when an argument is made that is related to a question of governmental policy, the layman, as emotions rise, begins to lose his awareness of a spiritual influence." [18]

But conscience does not speak in a vacuum. There is no reality in conscience-in-general, but only in conscience concerning decisions made or to be made; and these are not

---

[17] Langdon Gilkey, *How the Church Can Minister to the World Without Losing Itself* (New York: Harper & Row, 1964), p. 81.

[18] David Lawrence, "Is the Clergyman Changing His Role?" *U. S. News and World Report* (April 19, 1965), p. 116.

limited to some separate sphere marked "spiritual" but are as broad as life itself. We cannot speak responsibly about God without speaking about the world in whose affairs he confronts us, and we cannot speak with ultimate meaning about the world and its issues without speaking about God.[19] The text becomes God's Word exactly at the points where it shows us the meaning of our lives in relation to our most fiercely contested issues.

Civil rights, armament, wars of liberation, social welfare, honest local government—men struggle with such issues, worry over them, seek answers to them in a host of other places: "at service club luncheons, in suburban living rooms, in country club locker rooms and porches."[20] Is the one setting in which they cannot be mentioned forthrightly to be that single place in our society where they can be set in the perspective of the Scriptures? Extra-marital ventures, kickbacks, shaded income tax returns, padded expense accounts, the sacrifice of one's children to some image of success—men are caught in the toils of these matters about which, one way or another, they are returning daily decisions. If they are to hear the Word of God, it needs to come home to them as interpretation of their inner history at such points as these.

Harvey Cox makes a fruitful contribution to our approach to this responsible handling of the Word, as he calls attention to the crucial nature of the semicolon in the sentence with which Mark keynotes the preaching of Jesus: "The time is fulfilled, and the kingdom of God is at hand; repent,

[19] Cf. Ebeling, *Word and Faith,* pp. 354-62.
[20] Gilkey, *How the Church Can Minister,* p. 82.

and believe in the gospel" (1:15).[21] "The time is fulfilled, and the kingdom of God is at hand"—that clear indicative points out something factual about the nature of the time in which men stood—and stand. It does not exhort, nor plead, nor command; it simply states. This is the situation; this is where we are. In the light of this situation, a clear outgrowth of it, linked as closely to it as a semicolon can bind it, comes the imperative: "repent, and believe in the gospel." What we need is semicolon preaching! This is the situation, this is where we stand, this is who we are; because of which we need to see ourselves in a new light, think in new directions, turn around, repent. "Should preaching be in the indicative mode, or the imperative?" homiletics literature has often asked. Neither all one nor all the other; it is called to state the plain indicatives of the situation in which God now confronts us, matched by the urgent imperatives of conscience.

Only his own personal dialogue with the Scriptures, faithfully pursued day after day, can enable the interpreter to fulfill this calling. In his own tryst with the Bible he must persistently press two questions: What is the honest truth of this passage in itself? What does it say *now, to me, in the situation in which I stand?* If he hurries to the second question before he has patiently worked his way through the first, he will deal with it fancifully, inaccurately, and so will have read the Bible without hearing the Word of God. If he tarries long with scholarly delving in the first, without really arriving at the second, he will know much about an

---

[21] *The Secular City* (New York: The Macmillan Company, 1965), p. 116.

ancient record but nothing at all about the Word of God to him. No discipline in the minister's life is as important, or—if one is to believe what ministers repeatedly say about themselves in classroom and conference—as much neglected as this daily tryst with the Word, not as a mine from which to dig sermon texts but as the place where each man for himself must hear the Word of God.

For the one place where we best learn to let the Word interpret human life is in the solitary wrestlings in which it interprets *us*. Some of our best sermons will be produced by later reflection upon the insights born of these vivid hours [22]; but we shall miss all the best that God can do for us in them if we come to them as professionals looking for something to preach and not as weak, hard-pressed, sinful men whom only God can make whole. Faithfulness in this tryst with the Word can go far toward making vivid our handling of the Bible as vital interpreter of our life, putting reality and disarming humility into our approach to "man as conscience," and so delivering us form the crisis of the pulpit.

Ezekiel's scornful picture of the professional prophets of his era has about it a ring of reality concerning a prime hazard of the minister's calling in any age: "when the people build a wall, these prophets daub it with whitewash" (13:10). The Hebrew word for *wall* in this scathing sentence is one which, in its use outside the Bible, meant a wall built of stones loosely heaped together with no cement to hold them. To whitewash such a wall might give it some appearance of solidity, but this would only aggravate the insecurity

[22] See chapter 4, especially pp. 98-99.

by inviting men to trust it beyond its competence. The personal and social infidelities of his time had made of society such an insecure and threatened wall, Ezekiel declared, and these prophets, doing nothing to correct or reveal its weakness, covered it over with whitewash. That can happen in any age. It does happen when preaching fails to speak directly to "man as conscience," and so to allow the text to become God's Word which lays bare the real meaning of our life.

Whenever this happens, says Roy L. Honeycutt, in a penetrating study of this passage,[23] three causal conditions are not far to seek: the false prophets have no real "word form the Lord," they have lost the clarity of their perception of right and wrong, and they suffer from a loss of conviction. Against the attack of these dangers, the minister's daily self-searching in the light of the Scriptures builds its ramparts. If his study of the Bible is primarily a professional workshop function, he will have no word from the Lord, for he will have heard none. No encounter in personal wrestling will have made the Bible a direct illumination of the meaning of his life, and so the text will not have become God's Word to him. That being true, he will more easily see issues of right and wrong within the shadows of the relativities that infect our society than in the searching light of the Scriptures. Because his own use of the Bible has become more a professional discipline than a nurturing of his own soul and a fight for his life in the face of besetting sins, it need be no surprise that the note of desperate conviction falls silent in his ministry.

[23] *Crisis and Response*, pp. 143-67.

MEETING GOD IN HIS ACTS

Debate as we may what we choose to call "the existence of God," the Bible has no interest in that question. In its living faith, not the existence but the *acts* of God are what matters. He creates, redeems, sanctifies. He is a God who *comes,* and his comings are momentous. "For thou, O Lord," exclaims the psalmist,

> For thou, O Lord, hast made me glad by thy work;
>   at the works of thy hands I sing for joy (Ps. 92:4).

Because he is such a God and our faith is such a faith, there is little in the Bible or the Christian message that matters until it *happens again.* To believe there is a God, or that he acted in certain recorded events, or that such and such doctrines about him are true, is not what it means to have faith. Only when we can say with the psalmist, "Thou . . . hast made *me* glad by thy work," does faith come to life in us. When God's comings in Israel become the ground plan of *our* life, the texts which tell of them become God's Word to us, show us who we are and who, by his grace, we can become. Interpretation which allows that to happen is vital preaching; its roots are always sunk in the soil of such encounter in the interpreter's own life.

The Word meets us at the crucial center of the conflict in which we stand. God has created us by his Word, but our separation from it and from him is death. His Word made flesh conquers sin and death, and our response to the Word is the gateway to new life. This theological reality, the main thread of the Bible's message, is written large over the news as it comes to us, day after day. When we make the identification, God has spoken his Word to us.

Consider one day's front page of a metropolitan evening paper.[24] The day on which this chapter was written brought news of a battle involving several thousand men on both sides, leading to deaths estimated from seven hundred to a thousand of the enemy. As if silence might reduce actuality, losses to our forces were not estimated. Another story reported that the war in Viet Nam was currently costing our government $16.5 million a day. Elsewhere on the page, though no connection with this vast investment in destruction was mentioned, appeared the leader to a story of unprecedented famine overtaking the world. Still another item gave the account of police massing their forces in one city neighborhood to "get under control once for all" the violence of two gangs of youth, one of which was said to number two hundred, who had terrorized a school district and threatened further bombing and burning.

These are crashing symptoms of the self-righteousness and disregard for one another that infect our common life. There may be a lighter symbol of it in another human interest story of a family who traveled for several hours and arrived at a distant city before they *noticed* that their seven-year-old boy had been left behind in a filling station!

Yet the word of life was also present. Played up on the same page was the funeral of an airplane pilot who, after a disabling collision aloft, landed his plane and saw most of his passengers to safety, quite deliberately giving his own life in the attempt to extricate the last trapped man from the burning wreckage. "I'm only here because he's gone,"

[24] *Chicago Daily News,* December 10, 1965.

one passenger said. "He gave us a second chance at life."
In the twentieth century or in the first, "the old cost of the
human redemption" remains the same—a life laid down that
others may have a second chance.

We cannot speak God's Word—only he can do that. But
in our study of the Bible, our searching of our hearts in
prayer, and our dialogue with our time, we can so bring
biblical events into contact with ourselves and our brother
men that God can take our words and use them to speak his
Word. Unless our ministry is about that crucial errand, it
is about nothing much that matters. But if the Word is alive
only when it lights up the meaning of someone's life, far
more is at stake than getting it said. It must be *heard*. As
miraculously as wave motion in the ether is changed to nerve
impulses from ear to brain, and then from such physical
phenomena to conscious meaning that makes a difference
to us as spiritual beings, the word spoken must find its way
into the depths where it first *illumines* our experience and
then *alters* it. To this miracle of hearing, and the fascinating
demands it lays upon those who preach the Word, we must
address ourselves in chapter three.

For Further Study

1. The interpreter's depth and clarity of conviction
about the meaning of revelation is crucial. This chapter
has sought to deal with a most salient aspect of that subject,
but a study of *The Meaning of Revelation,* by H. Richard
Niebuhr (New York: The Macmillan Company, 1941) can
be immensely helpful. So, too, can *The Authority of the*

Bible, by C. H. Dodd (Torchbook ed.; New York: Harper & Row, 1958). *Theology and Preaching,* by Heinrich Ott (Philadelphia: The Westminster Press, 1965) can help the preacher know the ground he stands on. Dwight E. Stevenson's *The False Prophet* (Nashville: Abingdon Press, 1965) will help him find his way in what we have called today's crisis in preaching.

2. The study of sermons by master preachers can be of great benefit in learning to preach ably—if we know what we are looking for, and if what we are looking for is not principally material we can borrow! Take any sermon of Helmut Thielicke's and search it for the way in which he lets biblical characters hold the mirror to us. You might use his book *The Waiting Father* (New York: Harper & Row, 1959) for the purpose. Or, to observe how ably he does the same thing with material from Genesis, see *How the World Began* (Philadelphia: Fortress Press, 1961).

3. Can you put some of your thinking about these things to work in creating sermon ideas? What about a sermon on the battle into which life plunges us—with God fighting for our salvation—taking its stand on one of the scripture passages briefly noted on pp. 44-46? Or could you take one of the texts in which Paul says "my" (p. 48) as the foundation for a sermon on how God speaks to us through the Bible? Or John 20:24-29 (p. 49) could lead into a strong sermon on this subject.

3

The Miracle of Hearing

On Hearing Hangs Salvation

"Faith," wrote Paul at the climax of his normative statement of the theology of preaching (Rom. 10:5-17), "comes from what is heard, and what is heard comes by the preaching of Christ." We who preach do well to remember what is crucial here: not what is *said*—"proclaimed," as today's popular phrase has it—but what is *heard*. Responsibility is divided. Some rests with the hearer. Some we can leave in God's hands, since the Word spoken, when it really matters, is his Word; so that of our preaching we can pray, "I thank thee that my work ends and thy work begins." [1] But if the Word is to be truly heard it must be fitly spoken. The miracle of hearing is ever a primary concern of the preacher.

To hear is difficult. How little we hear one another in our daily round has impressed and often appalled our sensitive artists. A haunting scene in Thornton Wilder's *Our Town* brings Emily back from the dead, privileged to relive one day of her earthly life. Having chosen her twelfth birthday, she enters a scene of flurried activity in which her mother bustles about, full of plans and preparations for the festival occasion. Allowed only this precious day, Emily hungers for some real interchange. "Oh, Mama," she cries, "just look at me one minute as though you really saw me." But there is no slackening of the busy pace to allow for personal perception. Presently Emily exclaims, "I can't go on. It goes so fast. We don't have time to look at one another." Returning to the community of the dead, she sighs, "That's all human beings are! Just blind people." To which another of that company replies, "To be always at the mercy of one self-centered passion, or another . . .—that's the happy existence you wanted to go back to." [2]

Such blindness is part and parcel of our deafness. It stems from the same root—"to be always at the mercy of one self-centered passion, or another." There is more than prophetic irony in Isaiah's oracle of a people hardened and dulled by the unheard Word:

[1] John Doberstein, ed. *Minister's Prayer Book* (Philadelphia: Fortress Press, 1959), p. 50.
[2] Act. III.

> "Hear and hear, but do not understand;
> see and see, but do not perceive."
> Make the heart of this people fat,
>   and their ears heavy,
>   and shut their eyes;
> lest they see with their eyes,
>   and hear with their ears,
> and understand with their hearts,
>   and turn and be healed (Isa. 6:9-10).

The same insensitivity burdened Jesus, calling forth some of his most taut words of warning. Not once, but repeatedly, he concluded crucial sayings with his ominous, "If any man has ears to hear, let him hear." "Take heed what you hear," he admonished; "the measure you give will be the measure you get, and still more will be given you. For to him who has will more be given; and from him who has not, even what he has will be taken away" (Mark 4:24-25). Real hearing is cumulative. Those who take in and make their own even a little are in position to understand more. But deaf heedlessness, too, is compounded, leaving a man less and less able to make heads or tails of the decisive issues that daily pass him by.

Who dares turn indifferently from a matter so momentous to our Lord? Before we are *interpreters* of the Word, we are sinful men who stand in desperate need to *hear* it. On our hearing hangs our own salvation. But we are charged with the pastoral care of God's people, and our hearing of their need is crucial to that ministry. Nor can we *interpret* a Word we have not first attentively *heard;* it is our occupational hazard that we are speaking men and may be so driven by the question, "What shall I say?" that we find little time to ask, "What is God saying?" The waggish cynic warns, "Engage brain before opening mouth," but for us who preach it is more essential to engage the inner ear. Recalling the psalmist's plea (Ps. 95:7), the Letter to the Hebrews reiterates three times over,

> Today, when you hear his voice,
> do not harden your hearts (3:7, 15; 4:7),

and to our threefold need—as persons, pastors, and preachers—that comes home with telling force.

To one aspect of hearing, however, a peculiar solemnity attaches. If the failure to hear can be as disastrous as the Scriptures keep declaring, we dare not spare any pains to make hearing possible. How often has our utterance been so cloudy or distorted that men could not hear? How often has it been so drab and colorless that men thought it not worth hearing? How often have men turned from our interpretation of the Word more than ever confirmed in their own godless ways? How can our preaching make the problem of spiritual acoustics less acute? How, so far as it lies within our human power to do so, can we help accomplish the miracle of hearing?

BORN OF THE WORD

For one thing, we can give studious attention to the dynamic nature of language. Students of the matter are increasingly reminding us that there is something *active* about a word. Ernst Fuchs speaks forcefully of "language event"

65

and Gerhard Ebeling of "word event" in their penetrating discussions.[3] It is the province of a word, Fuchs says, to "admit" us to one area of experience or another. "For it is not true that man has given birth to language. Rather man is born out of language."[4] That this is true not only of the race itself, all that is uniquely human in us emerging with our capacity to articulate thought in words, but of individuals as well, the rise of Helen Keller to personhood makes startlingly clear. "Deaf, blind, mute . . . She is like a little safe, locked, that no one can open," says a perceptive observer in William Gibson's revealing play about her release from the silent dark of a subhuman childhood.[5] But she was more than a little safe that no one could open; she was a little animal that no one could reach—until Annie Sullivan found the way. Asked, "What will you try to teach her first?" Annie replied: "First, last, and—in between, language."[6] "She has to learn," Annie declared, "that words can be her *eyes,* to everything in the world outside her, and inside too, what is she without words? With them she can think, have ideas, be reached."[7] Endlessly, night and day, spelling *words* into the palm of Helen's hand, heroically struggling to forge the associative link with *things,* Annie declared to her unhearing charge: "one word and I can—put the world in your hand."[8] Who can forget the emotion packed moment of emerging personhood when Helen

---

[3] Note their essays in *The New Hermeneutic.*

[4] Quoted by Robinson, "Hermeneutic Since Barth" in *The New Hermeneutic,* p. 50.

[5] *The Miracle Worker* (New York: Bantam Books, 1962), Act I, p. 18.

[6] *Ibid.,* p. 30.

[7] *Ibid.,* Act III, p. 101.

[8] *Ibid.,* p. 104.

at last comprehended the bond of identity between the water flowing from the pump and the word spelled into her palm? Or the wonder of the quick capacity to make genuinely human response to persons as her eagerly extended hand received enough words to permit her first real communication? In a sense far more than figurative, her "being had emerged from language." [9]

How can we mouth the airy dismissal, "Words are cheap"? To say "brother" to another is to affirm that relationship and let it *be* what it is.[10] "Brother Saul," said Ananias (Acts 22:13), thus admitting the persecutor to the intimate bond of the Christian fellowship. "Saul was a brother according to theological jargon," men say in deprecation, "but not in the actualities of bloody human affairs!" Could theological insight have advanced to flesh and blood relation without the *word* to affirm it? What if no Ananias had dared to go with outstretched hand and affirming word? How desperately different might the world's history have remained for these two thousand years! There was every reason to distrust and fear this man—little to support the notion that this Saul was a "brother." But the word let the relationship *be* what in God's sight it was.

Words can be cheap when we use them cheaply. How vastly different is "brother" in the sentence, "If a brother or sister is ill-clad and in lack of daily food, and one of you says to them, 'Go in peace, be warmed and filled,' without giving them the things needed for the body, what does it profit?" (James 2:15-16). Such a word does not admit the brother

---

[9] Fuchs, quoted by Robinson, "Hermeneutic Since Barth," p. 55.
[10] *Ibid.*, p. 58.

to the true relation. It is not word-*event*. It has come loose from its moorings in experience.

God's Word, however, never loses this connection. Event is its essence. It creates. It saves. It has analogies in human experience which let us see its power. Love comes to its full existence only when it is spoken. The lover who adores in silence, even though devoted acts may fill the years, leaves something lacking in the full interpersonal reality of the relationship. In like manner, the man who lives through long years in the sunlight of God's providence enters a new relation when at last his heart *hears* that "God so loved the world that he gave his only Son, that whoever believes in him should not perish but have eternal life" (John 3:16). When something deeply wounding has come between husband and wife, or father and son, it is not enough for them to try to pick up the old relationship by being jovial, helpful, and even deeply faithful with each other. Words must be spoken: "I'm sorry!" which admit to real fellowship. As, in our relation to God, we need not only an about face in deeds, but articulate verbal confession in response to the Word: "Repent, and believe in the gospel" (Mark 1:15). Conversely, forgiveness is less than full restoration while two people try only to *act* toward each other as if no rift had ever opened between them. Before the bond is knit strongly again, words must both ask and grant forgiveness. So said Luther of God's Word: "If a hundred thousand Christs had been crucified and no one said anything about it, what use would that have been? Just betrayal to the cross. But when I come to this we must draw this deed into history and divulge it to the whole world. . . . To the deed must be added the use made of

68

the deed, that it may be proclaimed by the Word, held by faith and that he who believes may be saved." [11]

Paul recognizes the necessity that word ratify deed. "All this is from God, who through Christ reconciled us to himself and gave us the ministry of reconciliation," he writes; "that is, God was in Christ reconciling the world to himself, not counting their trespasses against them, and entrusting to us the message of reconciliation. So we are ambassadors for Christ, God making his appeal through us. We beseech you on behalf of Christ, be reconciled to God" (II Cor. 5:18-20). Something *done* through Christ comes first, but it is not complete until Word has conveyed and ratified act.

This is the nature of God's Word: it is Word-event. We are prisoners of sin and death, released by the Word. For a prisoner is not *free* when his cell door is left unlocked and unguarded. He may walk out, but he lives the ambiguous life of the fugitive, feeling hunted even when no one watches him, not in prison but not really free. Before freedom is his, a word must reach him: "acquitted," "pardoned," "justified." Is this not our case, until the Word reaches us? Through Jesus' act the prison doors are unlocked, but we are not fully free until the saving Word, heard deep within us, gives life.

It is tragically possible for the preacher to lose this life-giving bond between word and event. "We are suspended in language, which is a swift and powerful shorthand for communicating enormous chunks of reality," writes Michael Drury; "and it is easy to fall in love with the shorthand, thinking that by saying the word, we have invoked the reality beneath." [12] It is for this reason that one yearns for some

---

[11] Quoted by Gustav Wingren, *The Living Word*, p. 65n.
[12] *McCall's Magazine* (October, 1965), p. 101.

homiletic equivalent to the pure food and drug act, to require that the "manuals" and "annuals" now widely advertised for busy preachers carry the label, "Poison." For they make it too probable that ministers who use them will have the language shorthand with little of "the reality beneath." They cause word and event to come unstuck. Equipped with their offerings, the minister needs no costly delving in the Word, no struggle with his people's needs, no patient listening for the voice of the Eternal as he searches his own heart. Miss Drury recalls the remark of the physicist Niels Bohr, that "his great problem was never to speak more clearly than he could think." It is the minister's problem as well.

Words that admit men to great ranges of experience must be constantly involved with *events,* with resistant *things,* with confused and confusing *persons.* At the opposite pole from such earthy concreteness are the statements which issue from church conferences and ecumenical gatherings. What they say may be crucially important when translated into language which renews the association with the feelings and acts of persons, but in their shorthand they remain colorless and cold because they have said too much, too abstractly. Perhaps they must. Like the theological, philosophical, and scientific books the minister reads, they have the problem of making statements that will apply over wide areas and in varied conditions. It is the preacher's business to wrestle with them until he knows what they mean in the specific circumstances which confront him and his people, and to interpret them in relation to one vividly perceived area of our life. Only so can men *hear* what they are saying, and be "admitted."

Preaching is word-event which calls the church into being.

One must beware of overloading the passing phrases of scripture, but in the swiftly moving narrative of Luke, where no words are wasted, is it without significance that the account of Jesus' Nazareth sermon is prefaced with the observation that "He opened the book" (4:17)? How fully that accords with the disciples' exclamation at Emmaus: "Did not our hearts burn within us while he talked to us on the road, while he opened to us the scriptures?" (Luke 24:32). His teaching opened the book of the Old Testament, throwing a flood of light upon its meaning. Even more, his life, death, and resurrection opened the book, for he was himself the Word made flesh. It is still this opening of the book which calls the church into being, admits it to its own reality, lets it *become* what by God's call it *is*. This is our mandate to give first priority to our call as interpreters: it is this word-event which makes an audience into a congregation, a mere assembly into a church.

Preaching is word-event which brings faith to birth. "Faith," said Paul, "comes from what is heard." Faith is the Word becoming effective in us. This is why no one of us can achieve faith for himself, but must be given faith by the grace of God. Faith is not our creation. It is not self-generated. It comes in response to the Word. And since God gave the Word, faith is God's gift. But our witness to the Word needs to be credible. It needs to touch men's lives in ways that evoke the glad, surprised, "So that is what it all means!" Is it likely that we shall often achieve such credible witness if, at the end of crowded days, loaded beyond capacity with more worthy and important activities than our human strength can bear, we recognize that we *also* have a sermon to preach, and make what preparation we can in the time that

71

is *left*? The word-event which admits men to faith deserves better of God's ministers.

Preaching is word-event which proclaims as current reality what the text proclaimed to men of another time. It goes beyond recital of what once was said or done, to become fresh, direct address which arrests us and puts our lives in question. It is thus that our Lord's visit in the Bethany home of Martha and Mary (Luke 10:38-42) comes home to us. The word-event in which God encounters us here can allow little time for embroidering the narrative. "What happened?" "Why?" "What did it mean?" are not the questions that cry for attention. Nor will much that is significant word-event come of moralistic exhortations based on inferences from the behavior of Martha, or Mary, or both. Rudyard Kipling's lines on "The Sons of Martha" enter into the overworked debate concerning their relative merits. It is easy to see where the poet's sympathies lie, as he writes:

The Sons of Mary seldom bother, for they have inherited that good part,
But the Sons of Martha favor their Mother of the careful soul and the troubled heart.

Attending the gears and switches, moving mountains by their feats of engineering, splicing wires and harnessing waters, they give faithful service night and day. Concluding his account of them, Kipling observes:

And the Sons of Mary smile and are blessèd—they know the Angels are on their side,
They know in them is the grace confessèd, and for them are the Mercies multiplied.

They sit at the Feet—they hear the Word—they know how truly
the Promise runs.
They have cast their burden upon the Lord, and—the Lord He
lays it on Martha's Sons! [13]

But the gospel is neither a collection of edifying tales
told about Jesus and his friends for their biographical and
human interest, nor an anthology of practical maxims dealing with such matters as the relative merits of being a good
worker or a good listener. Why does Luke include this story
in his Gospel? Is not Raymond Roseliep close to the heart
of the matter in the closing lines of his "Summer Night at the
Koehens"?

> Martha busy in
> her kitchen sets a place mat
> for a guest not god.[14]

"Martha was distracted with much serving" (Luke 10:40),
and so are we. Sure that "Christ has no hands but our
hands," we set out to "build his kingdom." Our cluttered
service agenda supply their own evidence that we have "set
a place mat for a guest not god." He depends on us, more
than we on him! If we were to falter, his enterprise would
fail. Is that—*God*?

"Mary . . . sat at the Lord's feet and listened to his teaching" (Luke 10:39). What can we do that matters until we
have done that? Of what worth is our *doing* until we have

[13] From *Rudyard Kipling's Verse, Definitive Edition*. Reprinted by
permission of Mrs. George Bambridge, Doubleday & Company, and The
Macmillan Co. of Canada.

[14] *Commonweal*, December 11, 1964. Reprinted by permission of *Commonweal*.

heard? Are we like the little girl whose father found her sitting at his desk, surrounded by a clutter of scattered papers and spilled ink, who smiled proudly as she said, "I'm doing your work, Daddy"? How much of our busyness can stand scrutiny as *his* work? The man in the parable, who built his house on rock, was like one "who hears these words of mine and does them" (Matt. 7:24), but the *hearing* had to precede the *doing*. Nor is hearing a mere catching of a wisp of half-understood suggestion while we are in flight to do something we think important. To hear him thus is to hear him as "a guest not god." To God full attention is the least we can give.

Peter's last hours with Jesus (Mark 14:26-42) were an active man's tribute to "a guest not god." Hear him vow that he will never fail his Lord. See him sleeping in the garden while Jesus prays. Watch his reckless rush to Jesus' defense with a sword. Are these incidents, all pointing to Peter's assumption that Jesus was more dependent on him than he on Jesus, unrelated to the final ignominy of his denial? Only when we have let Jesus do for us what God alone can do, can our service be of any worth in his hands. Then his Word, to us and through us, can perform its dynamic ministry as the Word-event that admits to life.

MINISTRY OF CREATIVE DISTURBANCE

The role assigned to us in the miracle of hearing calls for a ministry of creative disturbance. Crucial change is seldom serene. Not without reason did adolescence, with its metamorphosis from childhood to adulthood, become known as the period of storm and stress. A revolutionary idea can strike a man or a society with earthquake impact. When a patient in psychotherapy is making longest strides toward wholeness, his energies can be drained in turbulent emotion. And the classic conversions in the history of revivalism or the case studies of such psychologists as William James were typically stormy. To be changed by the Word is to be disturbed. Where there is real hearing there is creative disturbance.

Preaching has suffered much from the myth of placidity. Cherishing the illusion that worship is designed to soothe them into peace, men demand preaching that will slip smoothly into that pattern. In support of the myth they quote "Be still, and know that I am God" (Ps. 46:10), as if that one verse were the whole substance of worship, and in forgetfulness that the psalm makes the verse less a soothing word than a disturbing challenge to our human pretensions, against the background of a field strewn with our broken weapons. The myth is at least as old as Jeremiah, who accused the false prophets:

> They have healed the wound of my people lightly,
> saying, "Peace, peace,"
> when there is no peace (6:14).

It called forth Jesus' denunciation, "Do not think that I have come to bring peace on earth; I have not come to bring peace, but a sword" (Matt. 10:34). And it confronts us now in such determined stifling of the gospel's challenge as that of the minister in an area of racial conflict, who said: "Of course I am for brotherhood, but my chief business is to save souls. Now if I preach brotherhood, members will leave and

75

they will be lost. Therefore, in order to save them and keep them saved, I cannot preach brotherhood." [15]

Such thinking has fallen victim to the placidity myth. For in fact, these members, remaining undisturbed, *cannot* be saved. Refusing to disturb them, such a minister does not safeguard the gospel in their lives; he makes sure that they will not even *hear* it. Not only does such fearfulness foreclose the proper facing of issues that might be growing points; it makes the whole range of the gospel so undisturbing as to be utterly uninteresting. Unbroken placidity is the formula for boredom.

Preaching, like the arts, can achieve its effectiveness by creative disturbance. Hear Picasso: "I give a man an image of himself whose elements are collected from among the usual way of seeing things in traditional painting and then reassembled in a fashion that is unexpected and disturbing enough to make it impossible for him to escape the questions it raises." [16] To those of us nurtured chiefly in traditional representational art, the Picasso portraiture comes as a shock. Strange proportions, planes in mixed perspectives, bewildering distortions of our usual surface vision require long, studious reexamination if we are to catch anything of what the artist is attempting. But some of us have come from sessions in a gallery where we have given ourselves to the effort, surprised to discover how much more we see in the faces on the street because Picasso has disturbed our casual vision.

[15] Quoted by Theodore O. Wedel, "Is Preaching Outmoded?" in *Religion in Life,* XXXIV (Autumn, 1965), 546.
[16] Françoise Gilot and Carlton Lake, *Life With Picasso* (New York: McGraw-Hill Book Company, 1964), p. 72.

"I want to draw the mind in a direction it's not used to and wake it up," Picasso explained. "I want to help the viewer discover something he wouldn't have discovered without me. That's why I stress the dissimilarity, for example, between the left eye and the right eye. A painter shouldn't make them so similar. They're just not that way." [17] Is that not a fair characterization of the role of the interpreter of the Word? The incongruities between our life and the gospel call do not justify our smooth preaching of untroubled and seldom troubling sermons.

There is seminal suggestiveness for the preacher in Picasso's solution to a problem in portraiture. Working on a painting which remained placid and lifeless despite all he could do, he experimented in a variety of ways with the possibility of combining in the composition a lithograph of the same subject. When finally he hit on the exactly right place and angle at which to hang it on the canvas, it was "like opening a window in the painting and letting in another structure from another plane." [18] Between this and the double analysis which looks searchingly at the Scripture and then at our affairs, formulating its theme and message from the tension between them, the analogy is instructive.[19] The Bible's message and our affairs do not easily harmonize; they meet more often in mutual challenge than concord. To superimpose Scripture upon our life, or our life upon the Scripture, is like "opening a window . . . and letting in another structure

[17] *Ibid.*, p. 60.

[18] *Ibid.*, p. 122.

[19] As a key concept guiding the preacher's approach to both biblical and contemporary subject matter, double analysis is given careful attention in my *Preaching to the Contemporary Mind*, pp. 41-45, 96-99, and in *Living Doctrine in A Vital Pulpit*, pp. 41 ff. See also pp. 20-26 above.

from another plane." But it is then that the dull, flat portrayal comes alive.

"Tell me the stories of Jesus," pleads the song; but the stories, told in unbroken first-century perspective, seldom help men *hear* the gospel. "Make the gospel relevant," runs our current cliché; but if that calls us to see things only in contemporary perspective, it makes the pulpit a commentator's rostrum—lacking teams of experts that give authenticity to the network commentators. It is the pulpit's peculiar assignment to open windows in our flat landscapes and disturb us by letting in another structure from another plane, which shows our tawdry and threatened life for what it is. When the pulpit gives too exclusive attention to either the first century or the twentieth, it cannot help men *hear* the Word.

We have seen that "man as conscience" is a basic principle of interpretation, enabling men to enter into the biblical message as the story of their lives; but it is more. For address to conscience is the focal point of the creative disturbance which enables men to *hear*. Much has been made of the need to touch men at the point of their questioning concern, but a part of our human lostness is our insistent asking of the wrong questions. How can we begin with a false question and arrive at a true answer? As Gustaf Wingren asserts, the Bible claims "the right to formulate these questions itself. The Word loses part of its content when it is made to reply to questions other than those that spring from the Word itself." [20] Will men give the attention requisite to hearing if *their questions* are not taken seriously? Will there be au-

[20] *The Living Word*, p. 22.

thentic gospel to hear if the message is exclusively *keyed to* their questions? These are the horns of our communicative dilemma.

To which James Pike replies,

Isn't it possible to give ultimate answers to penultimate questions? We can often start with a penultimate question, and then give the ultimate answer. Our problem is to help our hearers see that the thing that is bothering them is really a deeper question than they themselves realize and thus see that the Christian answer is relevant and connected—and will take them further even than they have wanted to go.[21]

In a notable sermon based on this principle, Pike began with the then current book and motion picture, *On the Beach,* and the questions concerning nuclear disaster which it made articulate. Not taking this lightly—for there is something not far short of ultimate in the magnitude of this threat—he went beyond it. The deeper, more personal question, he pointed out, is the question of death and of how we meet its challenge. The author of *On the Beach* had subsequently died, though not of nuclear radiation. This massive threat makes more dramatically insistent the question every man must face: How do you meet the demands death lays upon you?

To move thus from the penultimate to the final will involve that address to conscience in which the Word interprets us, plunging us into creative disturbance. All men, including us who are in the Christian fellowship, stand in some degree outside the gospel's way of looking at our life.

[21] *A New Look in Preaching* (New York: Charles Scribner's Sons, 1961), p. 38.

Having espoused the faith, we easily assume that our ideas and purposes stand in accord with it. The problem of the preacher is to help men see that God's call is still a call to repentance and growth, demanding radical change. To preach vitally is to plunge men into this crisis of change.[22]

Is it probable that we shall disturb men if we are not concrete and specific? To allude once more to Picasso, his sardonic mirth at the caution of a fellow artist calls forth recollections of some of the sadder and weaker hours of the pulpit. As young men, he and his colleagues in the surrealist movement had adopted a convention of denouncing varied aspects of the current culture, making pointed the dissatisfaction from which their creative endeavors stemmed. Their provocative challenges took such form as the shout, "Down with the army! Down with France!" One of their number, however, seemed far less disturbing with his cry, "Down with the Mediterranean." When queried about it, he explained, "The Mediterranean was the cradle of our whole Greco-Roman culture. When I shouted 'Down with the Mediterranean.' I was saying, 'Down with everything we are today.' " [23] The gospel's call to repentance is indeed a challenge to "everything we are today," but the generalization neither disturbs nor saves. The ultimate concern must reach us in terms of penultimate issues which are local, timely, and personal.

No interpreter can achieve omniscience concerning the sins, doubts, and temptations which challenge the gospel in the lives of his people; but methods are at hand by which he can

[22] I have developed this thesis and some of its practical implications in detail in my *Preaching to the Contemporary Mind,* pp. 66-81.
[23] *Life with Picasso,* 195-96.

know the tension points with enough accuracy to put realism into his message. The pastor who faithfully calls among his people, gives himself to a counseling ministry, and puts before him on his sermon worksheets some note of the needs he has currently sensed in the parish, will have abundant help to this end.[24]

Some ministers go beyond this to pastoral dialogue explicitly addressed to the formulation of the sermon. In a large suburban church whose congregation included numbers of workers in almost every vocational field, a series of sermons on Christianity in daily work gained vitality from such dialogue.[25] Dealing with advertising and public relations, medicine and the healing arts, communications, and a wide variety of other occupations, the sermons brought helpful insight into the Christian struggle in specific vocational arenas. Some weeks in advance of each sermon, the minister called together members of the congregation employed in the field of labor to be considered. In a first session they discussed the problems of the Christian so employed, and in a second they searched their Bibles together in an attempt to understand what Word might come to them within their concrete area of endeavor. Before the sermon was preached, a spokesman for the vocational group made a five-minute statement about the problems as the group understood them. Out of this creative interchange came preaching both specific and Christian.

In another parish a minister meets weekly with a rotating group of men of the church to discuss the preparation of the

[24] See chapter 1, pp. 20-21.
[25] Preached by Dow Kirkpatrick in the First Methodist Church, Evanston, Illinois, winter and spring 1965.

sermon to be preached three weeks later. A dozen representative men are recruited by a lay leader for a period of weeks so staggered that the group always contains some who have had experience in the process and others who have come freshly to it. The minister opens the discussion by stating the theme on which he believes he ought to preach and the Scripture lesson from which it is derived. All turn then to their Bibles for joint study of the lesson, sharing their insights from it. "What does this mean in our situation?" the minister asks, and the men contribute their understandings of problems and convictions it calls forth, as well as illustrative incidents from their experience. It is understood that the minister is not obligated to base his sermon on group consensus and that the word finally preached is his responsibility. Out of this process comes a flood of fresh insight into the human situation to which the Word speaks.[26]

Devices will vary, but the need is constant: the interpreter must find the human specifics to give his message the power of creative disturbance to awaken hearing.

POWER OF A LIVING IMAGE

Translation of the message into living images is a vital part of the preacher's role in the ministry of hearing. Jesus won a hearing for his message in no small part by the vividness of its embodiment in the parables. The theological understanding of myth as "that expression of the creative imagination which interprets the real in terms of the ideal,

[26] Justus E. Olson employs this method at the First Methodist Church of Beloit, Wisconsin. As now practiced in that parish, it represents the refinement of Dr. Olson's work with it over a twenty-year period, first among students at the University of Wisconsin and later in the First Methodist Church of Wausau, Wisconsin.

punctual events in terms of continuous situations" [27] lays stress on the power of the image to say what propositional statements cannot express. Thus the first eleven chapters of Genesis fasten structural elements of the Bible message tenaciously upon the mind. Experiments with a traveling theater doing vigorous and provocative drama for culturally deprived audiences in the rural South aim at "a structuring of experience so that the audience, once having seen itself and the world, has patterns to think with." [28] This perennial role of the living image lays its mandate on the interpreter of the Word.

Preaching on "The Expulsive Power of a New Affection," Thomas Chalmers fulfilled this ministry, as have the memorable preachers of every age. Taking as his text I John 2:15, "Love not the world, neither the things that are in the world. If any man love the world, the love of the Father is not in him" (KJV), Chalmers made a fresh restatement of the gospel. Using none of the familiar language of salvation by grace through faith, or of law and gospel, he preached on that theme with power which gripped men at the turn of the nineteenth century and still lingers today. Setting out to show that, "from the constitution of our nature," demonstrations of "the world's vanity" are incompetent to rescue us, but the love of God has power to do so, he stated the case by vigorous examination of human motives. Much of the language is outmoded, and the sermon seems long and heavy by today's standards; yet its psychological insight is still

[27] T. H. Gaster, "Myth," *The Interpreter's Dictionary of the Bible* (Nashville: Abingdon Press, 1962).

[28] Richard Schechner, "A Free Theater for Mississippi," *Harper's Magazine* (October, 1965), p. 34.

sound, its theology timeless. As vital as anything in the message, however, is the vivid image of "the expulsive power of a new affection" suggested in its title. It is the preacher's perennially new assignment to do for successive generations what Chalmers did for his, not only by the vigor of his argument but by the power of that image.

In this task creative literature has much help to offer. Consider a single instance, as Job asks our question, "Why are not times of judgment kept by the Almighty?" (Job 24:1). Death snatches one we desperately need. Telltale symptoms in one's own body fill him with dread as he waits the doctor's diagnosis. Secret despair lays its icy hand upon us. Why? Are we in the hands of some blind fate? Has God lost his power, or forgotten his love? What answer is there to the accuser in *J.B.*?

> If God is God He is not good,
> If God is good He is not God.[29]

It is easy for religious people who are not caught in these crushing toils to quote Job's words, "I know that my Redeemer lives, and at last he will stand upon the earth" (Job 19:25). But what can these pious words mean to one who must walk this bitter road?

To grasp the power of Job's answer, we must catch the torment of his question. Franz Kafka's novel, *The Trial*, puts Job-like anguish into fresh figures. There is something strangely like Job's suffering in Joseph K.'s perplexity—ar-

[29] Archibald MacLeish (Boston: Houghton Mifflin Company, 1958), Prologue, p. 14. Reprinted by permission.

rested for an undesignated crime, held subject to an inaccessible court, vainly demanding the right to confront his accuser, told not to hurt his chances by pleading his innocence. Just so inexplicable were the sorrows that fell on Job, just so unjust the certainty of his friends that his guilt was self-evident. And just so it seems to some of us. Though Joseph K. could not get a hearing in the court, he found its functionaries everywhere—and always disreputable. The court painter portrayed Justice with combined features of the hunter and the winged victory—sordid justice indeed! And the proceedings of the court were entirely incomprehensible.

Is that not how it was with Job? Hear his lament at the carelessness of God:

> It is all one; therefore I say,
>   he destroys both the blameless and the wicked.
> When disaster brings sudden death,
>   he mocks at the calamity of the innocent (Job 9:22-23).

What a frightful and frightening picture! God jeers at the tragedy! The Hebrew word used here "suggests the stammering, chuckling derision of brutal and half-idiotic mirth." [30] There is no answer to his cry,

> But I would speak to the Almighty,
>   and I desire to argue my case with God (Job 13:3).

Good men admonish him not to plead his innocence, but to confess his guilt. God's supposed justice has strange evidence in the absurdities of the world.

[30] H. Wheeler Robinson, *The Cross in the Old Testament* (Philadelphia: The Westminster Press, 1955), p. 24.

85

> Yet God prolongs the life of the mighty by his power;
>> they rise up when they despair of life.
> He gives them security, and they are supported;
>> and his eyes are upon their ways. (Job 24:22-23.)

It is all absurdly without meaning. So says modern despair; so says Joseph K.; and so too says Job. Was Jesus entering into this universal hopelessness in his cry from the cross: "My God, my God, why hast thou forsaken me" (Mark 15:34)? Until we plumb the depths of Job's desperation in the face of this inaccessible God, we can make little of his conviction that his Redeemer lives.

The Redeemer to whom he refers cannot be simply identified with the Lord of the New Testament. His *gô'ēl* (redeemer) is the next of kin, who is bound to vindicate him in the face of his adversaries. But Job sees that figure in something like cosmic proportions, for he declares that, even beyond death

> I shall see God,
>> whom I shall see on my side,
>>> and my eyes shall behold, and not another
>>> (Job 19:26-27).

Is this a cosmic defender against God? Is it something in God himself—God defending him against God?

This faith held his life together when he might have gone down in final defeat. That we shall be so sustained is no foregone conclusion. It was not so for Joseph K. The priest told him a parable of a man who sought this inaccessible court and waited the remainder of his lifetime outside the door to which a forbidding guard denied him entrance. Just

86

before he died, it occurred to him to ask why, in all these years, with countless others also needing access to the court, no one else had sought to enter by this door. "Because," the guard told him, "this door was for you." What might have been the outcome if he had boldly attempted to enter, unintimidated by the guard? Have we, too, been too easily dissuaded?

It was not so with Job, whose desperate, protesting, courageous faith kept trying the door. It need not be so with us. We can try the door by prayer. We can beat upon it by commitment to the best we know in the face of bitter circumstance. We can put our weight against it by our witness to love—love as we have seen it in Christ upon his cross—in a world of hate. For that cross is our final hope. In the last moment of Joseph K.'s execution, he saw someone leaning toward him with outstretched arms from a high and distant window. The question of what that might mean flooded his mind in death with a last hope against hope. But we need not wonder so, for we have seen the Christ upon his cross. There is a Redeemer to stand up for us at last! Though there is much we cannot pretend to understand, we can say with Job, yet with a fullness of meaning that he—far on his other side of the Cross—could not know:

> I had heard of thee by the hearing of the ear,
>   but now my eye sees thee;
> therefore I despise myself,
>   and repent in dust and ashes (Job 42:5-6).

"Like a dog!" murmured Joseph K., as death claimed him. Was it more than our idiom for an ignominious death? Was it like a dog in falling victim to circumstance? Being shaped by the situation? Never entering the door meant for him? Missing the grace received by faith? It need not have been so. It was not for Job. Thank God, it need not be for us.

So the fresh images at hand in creative literature can answer to the haunting images of the Bible, and hearing the interplay between them we shall find ourselves interpreted and discover the power to waken men into hearing. But this struggle with the dark problem of Job has already suggested another aspect of the interpreter's task. There are passages in the Bible so difficult that we shun them, or so dark to us that we would not be spontaneously drawn to preach from them. Yet, when we wrestle with them, they often release some message we could not dare to have missed. Is there an orderly, dependable way of facing us to the many-sided richness of the Scriptures, that these treasures may have their chance to be heard? In the next chapter we shall seek to find the answer.

For Further Study

1. The theological dynamics of language merit the interpreter's careful attention. Ernst Fuchs delves creatively in this area, in his paper included in *The New Hermeneutic,* suggested for further study following chapter 1. Of great worth in pursuing this line of thought from other angles are *The Living Word,* by Gustaf Wingren (Philadelphia: Fortress Press, 1960) and *The Language of Faith,* by Samuel Laeuchli (Nashville: Abingdon Press, 1962). Books exploring the relation of creative literature to religious concern

and theological issues are so numerous that it may seem invidious to name only one. Especially apt in its suggestiveness, in pointing the relation of living images from the novel to scriptural insights, is *The Prophetic Voice in Modern Fiction,* by William R. Mueller (Anchor Books ed.; New York: Doubleday & Company, 1959).

2. You might find it profitable to begin work on a sermon which would make extensive use of an image from literature as an instrument to resharpen the focus on a biblical message. This can be richly rewarding, though it is not an easy device to employ. Not enough attention to the literary source, and you have only confusion and enigma for those not familiar with the book; too much, and instead of a sermon you have a book review with religious overtone. To avoid both dangers calls for hard, skillful work. To see it masterfully done, turn to the sermon on "Expiation" in *Sermons Preached in a University Church,* by George A. Buttrick (Nashville: Abingdon Press, 1959).

Now select your scripture and novel and go to work. This will be a sermon you should keep on the back burner for some weeks, letting it simmer slowly, before you rush it to the pulpit. If you do it patiently and with care, it may be a memorable experience for you and your people.

3. *The Trial,* by Franz Kafka (New York: Alfred A. Knopf, 1957) offers one possibility for this kind of sermon, and there are possible leads toward its development in the discussion on pp. 84-88. Need I say that it would be rash to attempt such a sermon merely on the basis of these remarks? You will want to study *The Trial* with care, and it would be useful to read Mueller's quite different interpretation of Kafka in *The Prophetic Voice in Modern Fiction.* If you

89

decide to base the sermon on material from Job, that biblical giant should have fresh study; and for that purpose, Paul Scherer's exposition in *The Interperter's Bible* will be briskly stimulating. Out of all this can emerge a *hearing* of the Word in Job that will linger long with you and with many in your congregation.

4. While the sermon suggested above simmers slowly, you might bring to a quicker boil an interpretation from Luke 10:38-42, possibly finding some of its provocation in the material on pp. 72-74. In preparing to let the Word-event speak currently through this scripture, not as recital of the past, it would be helpful to review what was said in chapter 1 (see especially pp. 26-32) about the distinction between *exposition* and *execution*.

5. Such creative dialogue in the sermonic process as is briefly suggested on pp. 81-82 will repay further investigation. The report of such a project is given in some detail in "Sermon Seminar in a Parish Church," *The Christian Century* (January 19, 1966), pp. 75-77. Closely related to such consultations in the *preparation* of the sermon are the various ventures in dialogue now being tried to complete the communication cycle by "feedback" after it has been preached. For an excellent brief handbook for such ventures see *A Listener's Guide to Preaching*, by William D. Thompson (Nashville: Abingdon Press, 1966).

4

Interpreter Under Orders

Initiative of the Word

"Week by week," writes J. W. Stevenson, "I had to make myself the arbiter of what would be read from God's Word, what would be asked for in prayer, what would be confessed, what would be remembered in thanksgiving, and in what words of psalm and hymn these people present before God would speak to him." The reflection was called forth by a parishioner's—probably exaggerated—ruefulness at the subjectivity of his faith and worship as compared with simple French peasants he had seen making their way to a parish church.

"We'd say it was fear and superstition," said the man regarding their motives.

But is it better to be a Protestant, and free from all superstition, and lie on your back on the hillside when the church bell is calling you? I watched these people touching holy water to remind themselves that they had to be saved. Is it better to be a Protestant and come and go easy-minded, and think you've no need of saving? There's been nothing to make me realize that we're all caught in a net and can't get out of it.[1]

Was his vunerability to the subjective heightened by a way of selecting scripture lessons and texts which left them too much to the minister's spontaneous understanding and preference?

How *are* texts to be selected? The minister who stands within a liturgical tradition is thereby guided to the appropriate lessons for any Sunday. Without presuming to debate the relative merits of a mandatory following of liturgical "propers," it may be noted that if the text interprets our life we need a wide range of lessons to put our self-understanding in adequate perspective. Depending on the Word to examine, mirror, judge, and guide us, we need nothing less than the full scope of the Scriptures to provide the biblical focus of the ellipse. Whether through the unfolding pageant of the liturgical year, or by some other means, the minister needs some method of making sure that the Bible itself has put his pulpit under orders.

As servant of the Word, he is sent not to speak his own wisdom, impress men by his cleverness, or captivate by his

---

[1] *God in My Unbelief* (New York: Harper & Row, 1963), pp. 121-22.

charm. Preaching as "the bringing of truth through personality" [2] takes all these personal factors conscript, yet it never
becomes what it was meant to be if these subjectivities of the
individual witness overshadow the massive objectivity of
the given message. Neither is the preacher called in order
that he may harp on one string of doctrinal or ethical enthusiasm, nor is it his mission to subject the Word to the role
of merely answering his people's questions, hunting texts
which permit it to speak dutifully when it is spoken to! The
Word has its own questions, which must not be shirked, lest
its horizon so contract that it cannot interpret our life from
its own eternal perspective.

In the biblical record nothing is clearer than the initiative
of the Word. So says Jeremiah: "The word of the Lord
came to me" (1:4). He did not seek it out; it claimed him.
So it is with prophet after prophet—"The word of the Lord
came to Ezekiel" (Ezek. 1:3); "The word of the Lord that
came to Hosea" (Hos. 1:1).; "The word of the Lord that
came to Joel" (Joel 1:1). In what clear sense can it be said
that the word of the Lord *came* to the preacher in today's
pulpit? Protestantism's central dependence on the pulpit as
the medium for contact with God through his Word makes
it imperative that the message arise from the initiative of
the Word as it *came* to the preacher, not the initiative of
the preacher as he made his own selection from the Word.

Some planned approach to the task of interpretation must
put the minister under the mandate of the Word. The lectionary, with its chosen lessons for the respective Sundays of
the year, is one obvious answer to this necessity; but it is not

[2] Brooks, *On Preaching*, p. 5.

the only one. There is the viable alternative of a wise use of the sermon course in which the preacher draws all his text material for a fairly extended period—usually about three months—from one book of the Bible, attempting to let the message of that book regulate the pulpit proclamation in a way that covers its main themes and types of material. Used with intelligent regard for the doctrinal emphases of the seasons of the church year, this method, too, can free the Word from the mandate of the preacher and place him under the command of the Word. Confronted thus with texts too hard for him, or too far from his personal predilections to have been his spontaneous choice, he will pay a price in a more demanding kind of preparation. But he will move at depths of interpretation not open to a message more simply keyed to texts that attracted his subjective response.

INTERPRETER AS RESPONSIBLE SPOKESMAN

Even for the minister not under the mandate of a fixed liturgical tradition, the lectionary—either used consistently throughout the year or followed in some of the seasons and abandoned for sermon courses from Bible books in others—can be a helpful guide. Almost every denomination now offers such a resource as at least an optional aid to the ordering of worship. Among the Old Testament lesson, the Epistle, and the Gospel designated for each Sunday, the minister is still given some latitude in selecting text material. In the use of the lessons he must determine whether to preach from a verse text, a paragraph, or a larger block of Scripture.[3] This freedom of choice, within the context of lessons carefully selected for the day, makes allowance for his human

[3] See chapter 5 for a discussion of these alternative textual forms.

capacity to respond, even while it puts him under orders from the Word.

Faithful, studious execution of the lectionary makes the interpreter *the spokesman of the gospel as the church has understood its unfolding sequence.* These lessons have been chosen against a background of experience wider than his own. They culminate a corporate attempt to give the church a full exposure to the whole sweep of the Scriptures. Within the denominational tradition they represent an informed selection of lessons which, season by season, give scope for the preaching of a message grounded in a theologically sound understanding of the gospel.[4] Repeating the cycle of readings from year to year, the minister is invited to explore their riches with growing comprehension of the depths within depths characteristic of the great scenes of the Bible. When minister and people are confronted by such cyclic repetition of the gospel as the church has understood its priorities, cumulative encounters cultivate the congregation's understanding and growth.

Preaching from a lesson sequence so chosen is designed to edify, in the New Testament sense: it *builds up the church.* Thus Paul says, "he who prophesies edifies the church" (I Cor. 14:4), and demands that ecstatic utterances be confined to those which can be interpreted by reason, "so that the church may be edified" (I Cor. 14:5). Or the Letter to the Ephesians recalls that God's gifts are "for building up

---

[4] The doctrinal orientation of the seasons of the church year, and their relation to corresponding elements of the New Testament *kerygma,* are subjects of no small import in an informed and creative use of the lectionary. Since I have written at length on this matter elsewhere, I do not treat it here, but refer the reader to my *Living Doctrine in a Vital Pulpit,* pp. 71-90.

the body of Christ" (4:12). The guidance of the lectionary
guards the church against the subjective enthusiasms of the
minister, or the corresponding blind spots in his understanding of the faith, which might render less balanced his presentation of the message. In the cycle of the church year it
presents the whole biblical message in rounded form. Because the lectionaries of the major denominations, drawing
from a common historical tradition, share large areas of cor-
respondence, the congregation whose services highlight these
readings is nurtured in a biblical point of view which grounds
its growing ecumenicity in its central acts of worship.

Using the lectionary as the basis of his choice of texts, the
minister has his private judgment buttressed by the historic
experience of the church and the responsible scholarship of
its more able interpreters. To make equally valid choices
of lessons, the individual minister would need talents and
resources open to few. The qualifications it would require
have been well stated by Charles W. F. Smith.

1. A knowledge of the Scriptures as a whole, such as
would enable him always to have in mind relevant passages
with an awareness of their relationship to each other;

2. An ability to organize and arrange the Scriptures for
use in a cycle that would afford the congregation a full and
rounded periodic presentation of the gospel and its application to a way of life;

3. A grasp of the problems presented by modern Biblical
study and the skill to present the positive contribution it
offers;

4. Freedom from preoccupation with a particular area or
application of the gospel and willingness to present aspects
of the Biblical *Heilsgeschichte* (story of salvation) with

which he feels less congenial but which are necessary to a fully rounded presentation; and

5. An awareness of contemporary pastoral needs that, brought to the analysis of the Biblical material, would produce a Christian understanding of those problems and prepare the way for an "evangelical" and "existential" solution.

"This," as Smith concludes, "is to ask too much of the preacher." [5] But such exorbitant demands need not be laid on the individual interpreter, since the church has placed the resources of the lectionary in his hands.

MANDATE OF A BIBLE BOOK

Even when he does not follow the lectionary, the minister may place himself under the mandate of the Word. Subjecting himself to the leading of a book of the Bible, he may "preach his way through" it as the basis of a course of sermons which provide the pulpit fare for a period of some twelve to fourteen weeks. Such an approach to the Scriptures provides opportunity for a genuinely cumulative teaching sequence. It allows the characteristic message and vital mood of a major book to reach the congregation with continuity that reinforces its impact. It teaches responsible methods of Bible study by example, as the minister, without academic discussion of exegetical and critical theory, regularly uses these methods in drawing treasures of interpretation from the selected book. It encourages members of the congregation to read their Bibles with more regularity and system than many would otherwise achieve. Practiced con-

[5] *Biblical Authority for Modern Preaching* (Philadelphia: The Westminster Press, 1960), pp. 55-56.

sistently for a part of each year, it cultivates a biblical point of view within the congregation. The sustained and orderly Bible study which it requires of the minister enriches his knowledge of the Scriptures, lending strength to his ministry in ways that extend far beyond the limits of the course in question.

Preparation for such a course begins long in advance, preferably at least in the preceding year. It will never be done with greater profit than when it is rooted in the interpreter's own devotional use of the Bible. For this purpose a devotional diary may prove fruitful, gathering the notes and reflections from consecutive daily study of a given biblical book. Taking one of the Gospels, for example, the minister reads from it each day the passage which advances him just one complete episode or unit of thought beyond the reading of the day before—a parable and its setting, a question asked and the teaching it brought forth, an incident in the ministry of our Lord. Recording the chapter and verse reference in his devotional diary, he then distills into succinct paragraphs the answers to the two questions which guide his meditation: What is the meaning of this passage within the Gospel? How does it speak personally to me? The first question leads him to careful exegetical study, the second to that self-examination without which the whole exercise remains academic and professional, achieving no personal encounter. Having recorded his responses to these questions, he may well conclude the meditation by lifting its concerns to God in prayer, keeping clarity and reality in his praying by compressing it into a few sentences in the diary.

Its primary value will inhere in the devotional diary's nurture of the minister's own spirit. Professionalized use of the Bible imposes a dangerous occupational hazard on the clergy. Busy search for sermons can eclipse personal encounter. When the minister reads his Bible, he must silence the *preacher* to save the *man*. Asking too hastily, "What can I preach about this?" he will produce sermons which lack the ring of reality. Between the vigor of his personal encounter and the authenticity of his preaching there is a direct relation. The better the minister succeeds in postponing the homiletic question in his devotional study, the more useful for subsequent sermon preparation will be the diary in which he records his reflections.

A year or more later, preparing to preach a course from the book which has spoken to his own devotions, the interpreter returns to his diary. As he rereads it, he discards much as too commonplace or too personal. In supplying his own contact with the Word, it has fulfilled its purpose on the day it was written. Here and there, however, he will come upon a page packed with significance that cries to be shared with his people. Such pages he will lift out for further study and reflection—both exegetical and pastoral—and these will become the seeds of sermons to be preached in the course. Because they retrace the encounter in which the study of the passage allowed the text to interpret the man, becoming God's Word to him, they possess the initial vitality to sustain the growth of sermons destined to precipitate this encounter for others.

This done, the preacher can go on to his more professional study of the book. Though he has delved in its backgrounds since his seminary days, he will give fresh reading to at least one or two scholarly treatises on it, refreshing and filling in his knowledge of its historical setting, its critical problems, and its unified message. He will reread the book in its continuity and make an outline of its contents. Out of this study some aspects of its encounter will come freshly to his attention, to be added to those already gleaned from his devotional diary.

The tentative list of passages calling for treatment, thus compiled, will probably prove too long for the weeks allotted for the course. In trimming the list to fit the time, he will bear in mind the necessity of making the course adequately representative of the main themes and types of material in the book. In this process he will turn to the commentaries to check his own interpretations of the respective passages against those of recognized authorities. This use of the commentary only after he has done his own diligent work on a given passage will enable the authorities to verify, correct, or amplify his work without stifling his ability to speak in "his own peculiar tone." To go to the commentary too soon is to invite the danger of becoming merely its echo. To neglect the commentary is brashly to presume on the adequacy of one's own unaided scholarship. To turn to the commentary at this point in the preparation is to enhance creativity by discipline.

The preparatory steps completed, the minister will proceed to the formulation of specific themes, stated as vigorously as he can contrive.[6] He will then correlate themes and calendar. In the nature of the preaching event each sermon, though it takes its place in the wholeness of the impact of the course, must be in itself an independent and in some measure complete encounter with the Word. This is true because it is the nature of the Word itself to speak to us fully of our

[6] Concerning the formulation of themes, see chapter 5, p. 126.

lostness and God's salvation at every point at which we enter into real dialogue with it. It is true also because of the empirical nature of preaching: though the course has continuity for the preacher and for some segment of the congregation, every sermon is heard by persons who missed what went before and will not hear what follows, but who nevertheless stand in need of the Word of God as he sends it to them on this important day.

It is not essential that the sequence of themes in the course follow the order in which the material stands in the Bible book from which it is preached. In ordering the sequence the minister will take other factors into account: the needs of pastoral care, the themes brought to mind by the procession of the church year, the special concerns which must be brought to focus on given occasions. When he has arrived at the order of themes best qualified to serve the needs of his parish at this particular season, he will set up a file folder, or a section of his notebook, for each sermon, for the accumulation of material and the refining of his thinking, and proceed week by week to the preparation.

Near the time of its beginning, he will announce the course to the congregation. Some ministers publicize the whole block of themes for the period to be covered—a practice which has the advantages of (a) indicating the seriousness with which the minister takes his work and expects his people to take it; (b) revealing by the current relevance of the themes the aim of the course to speak currently vital truth, not to dwell retrospectively on past proclamation; and (c) indicating to the congregation specific passages a fresh reading of which can supply background for fuller response to the Word on any given Sunday. Other ministers omit the listing of themes, believing that focal attention should center on the whole message of the book to be studied, not on the preacher's formulation of subjects.

In either case the minister will invite his people to read the book. He will say that during the specified period the sermons will deal with God's Word to us through the selected book, and worshipers will find a richer experience in worship by making this book an instrument of their daily devotions for these weeks. Not all the people will follow this suggestion (When do *all* the people respond to *any* invitation?), but a significant number will. Many will be helped to begin the practice of regular Bible reading, in a book made sufficiently meaningful by the Sunday services to encourage their continuation.

BOOK COURSE AND CHRISTIAN YEAR

Sermon courses thus carried out can be made to fit the needs of the liturgical year. Consider two possible course sequences by way of example. Suppose the minister were to preach a course on the Gospel according to Luke—what could provide richer material for Advent and Christmastide than Luke's first three chapters, with their poetic interpretation of the Old Testament hope and its fulfillment in the coming of Christ, their portrayal of the ministry of John the forerunner, and their beautiful narratives of the nativity? Universal Bible Sunday, second Sunday in Advent, might be observed in either of two ways. The sermon could deal with one of Luke's early passages redolent of Old Testament material, to show the unified wholeness of the Bible's central message, or a background sermon on the Gospel of Luke as a whole could celebrate the ministry of the Scriptures to us through the concrete examination of this representative book. The Epiphanytide theme—God's unveiling himself to all men through Christ—could then find abundant development through one of the passages in which Luke's stress on universalism is central. Luke's stories of our Lord's temptation and passion would guide a deeply meaningful pilgrimage through Lent, and the unique wonder of his resurrection chapter would climax the course on Easter Day.

Following this significant period with the Gospel of Luke, the congregation could be taken through the Acts of the Apostles in the remainder of Eastertide and the beginning of the Pentecost cycle. Such a sequel would recognize the literary unity of Luke-Acts and would aptly celebrate the Easter-Pentecost cycle. For here the living Christ—whose triumph and continuing presence highlights the weeks of Eastertide—is seen at work in his body, the church; here the Pentecost experience finds its fullest record; and here the witness of the Holy Spirit to an expanding world is seen in episode after episode.

Kingdomtide, from the last Sunday in August to the beginning of Advent, might be set as the time for preaching on one of the prophetic books—in this instance Jeremiah. The prophet's social struggle, his pointing forward to a new covenant, and his many resemblances to Jesus could supply a base for a memorable celebration of the themes most appropriate to this season.

Another year the minister might adapt a course sequence to its seasons differently, as would befit the books to be considered. Suppose he were to make Mark the Gospel for the year's study—he would find little Advent or Christmastide material and might begin the course on the Sunday after Epiphany, carrying it through Lent or possibly Easter Day. In the three months after Easter, I Corinthians might then be the basis of another course, fitting the season by its matchless interpretation of the Resurrection and its awareness of the living Christ and the work of the Holy Spirit in the midst of our mundane and sinful life. This sequence might well be preceded by a course on Deutero-Isaiah, beginning in Kingdomtide and continuing through Advent. Such a course would highlight these seasons by its social concern. It would point up God's acts in history, overriding the designs of men such as Cyrus and using Israel in ways beyond her knowledge or desire. It would find a fitting Advent climax in the Servant Songs which link the Old Testament hope with God's act in the Incarnation. Thus, from year to year, the minister can fit his interpretation of book after book to the celebration of the seasons and the enrichment of his people's encounter with the Word.

"How," men sometimes ask, "can such sequences be developed with meaningful continuity in the face of the many special occasions and concerns which claim a place in the pulpit ministry?" As we have seen, it is not required that we take up the material in any Bible book in its chapter and verse order. Given some freedom of adaptation to the calendar, there is material in any major book of the Bible to allow the Word to interpret our life in terms of almost any interest or issue that merits central attention in worship. To set these special occasions and interests within an established biblical context is to bring out their true meaning as a part of the life of the church more adequately than is probable in topical sermons. The minister who is attentive both to the

104

details of the Christian year and the habits of his denomination can anticipate virtually every special subject that should have attention in his pulpit in any year. His correlation of these subjects with the Bible book courses he is developing can make of them, not interruptions of orderly encounters with the Word, but demonstrations of the Scripture's pointedness in touching timely concerns.

Consider a few illustrative examples. It would be hard to hit upon a major book of the Bible which would not interpret our life in some aspect of the issues thrust forward by Race Relations Sunday. This falls in a season when, under either of the plans suggested above, a course from one of the Gospels would be in progress. Material thus under consideration might include such strands as our Lord's dealings with the culturally and pseudoracially estranged Samaritans. It might point to his concern for the *person,* which always transcended class, caste, or other grouping. Or it might highlight the universal inclusiveness of God's love to all men. Where these scriptural verities meet the issues that grow out of our hardness of heart in the racial conflict, vividly interpreting the meaning of an explosive aspect of our life, sermon themes are bound to emerge.

Many special occasions will have to do with what we once called the missions of the church and now more adequately conceive as the church in mission. So constant is this imperative in the Bible that almost any book under consideration will sound its call. Instances in the Gospels are obvious: our Lord's great commission; or his instructions to the disciples as he sent them out to preach, teach, and heal; or the implications of the "whosoever" of such passages as John 3:16, which make it clear that a gospel urgent here is urgent everywhere. Universalism in the Old Testament roots in God's covenant with Abraham—"By you all the families of the earth will bless themselves" (Gen. 12:3)—and is expanded in such books as Jonah and Ruth, written for no other purpose than to confront Israel with God's saving love for all peoples. There is the central fact of the Christian message, that through the death and resurrection of Christ God's victory over evil so changed the human situation that all men everywhere need to know of it. The completion of the victorious struggle in the Resurrection and Pentecost led, and still leads, to the existence of the church for the sole purpose of carrying the good news to all men.[7]

Other special causes will relate to the call to stewardship, never long absent from any major book of the Bible. God's sovereign ownership of all forces in history, the rights of the Creator in his creation, the sacramental nature of life in a world God has made, the obligation to share with others the love which has been freely given to us—these basic scriptural themes are the essence of the stewardship imperative. In most books they become almost painfully specific—as when Paul, hardly pausing for breath after the glorious spiritual climax of the Resurrection chapter, turns to its natural and inevitable consequence: "Now concerning the contribution for the saints" (I Cor. 16:1).

Beyond these issues common to all communions lie others peculiar to one's own denomination, often even more difficult to fit into the timetable of a projected Bible book course. Consider, for instance, the annual Commitment Sunday of The Methodist Church, when members are asked to

---

[7] This is emphasized repeatedly in *The Living Word,* by Gustaf Wingren. See especially pp. 28-29, 40-41.

pledge themselves to abstinence from alcoholic beverages. Seen as a special topical interest, this can be troublesome to the minister and can seem to many to be a legalistic expression of pietism antithetic to the gospel of grace. It need not remain in that orbit. It can properly come to the congregation in the context of the disciplined life of witness, in which the Christian as a "spiritual athlete" (I Cor. 9:25) puts himself under restraints which will enhance his witness to his Lord and avoid all that might call it in question or cast a shadow upon it. Abstinence takes its place in such consideration not as a legalistic requirement but as a natural consequence of Christian concern. This theme is no stranger to most major books of the Bible.

A course on almost any Bible book will lead to a facing of social responsibility. In this context the social liabilities of alcohol in the modern age—together with the contribution the Christian can make by renouncing participation in this complicating factor in all other social problems—is no deviation from the biblical line of march.

Or the minister may call attention to the implications of freedom in Christ. Here Paul points the way in such passages as Romans 14:13-23. The reasons for the Christian's abstinence lie far beyond fear of harm which his indulgence may bring to himself. "If your brother is being injured by what you eat," wrote Paul concerning the problem of food offered to idols, "you are no longer walking in love" (vs. 15). It takes little social sensitivity to understand the parallel to that situation in a society where millions who begin as casual social drinkers end as problem drinkers whose lives are needlessly marred by alcohol. If my brother is being injured by the example or social atmosphere created by my drink, I am no longer walking in love.

The minister who takes special subjects in stride as belonging to Bible courses carefully developed can more adequately present every theme he is required to treat. None of them need be regarded as detours from the Word as interpreter of our life. "The book to read," said James McCosh, "is not the one which thinks for you, but the one that makes you think. No book in the world equals the Bible for that." [8] Courses on Bible books will lend vigor to current thinking and fruitfulness to the annual cycle of preaching.

COMMANDED BY DIFFICULT TEXTS

Not least of the strengths which accrue when the Word puts the interpreter under orders is the unexpected richness discovered in the struggle to deal with themes the minister might otherwise avoid. Since space does not permit the exploration of all such themes, one must be allowed to represent the rest. The element of miracle presents itself so constantly in all parts of the Bible, with such attendant difficulties for many contemporary readers, that we turn to it by way of illustration.

The interpreter may seek to evade the problem raised for many minds by saying that his treatment of the miraculous deals with its spiritual implications, not the crass details of physical event. This, however, does not solve the problem. No matter how symbolically he treats the wonder stories, he must, at least by implication, adopt some stance with regard to the *happenings* they narrate. If he has no questions con-

[8] Virginia Ely, ed. *I Quote* (Westwood, N.J.: Fleming H. Revell Company, 1947), p. 28.

cerning the literal facts which underlie the account, he may
be sure that many in the congregation do; and these, for the
most part, will be the young and the uncommitted, to whom
a vital encounter can be most crucial. To bypass their questions is to inhibit their capacity to *hear* the real message the
interpreter is eager to convey. To shirk the necessity of facing such questions is to leave the uninstructed hearer without
guidance in his own Bible reading, with the result that he
may well lay the book aside as beyond his comprehension.

Nor is it enough to dismiss the matter with the hasty assumption that we must accept the literal factuality of the
wonder stories because the God who made the world *could*
do what he pleased with his creation. The listener may counter with a mental note that, regardless of what God *could* do,
this is not the way he has chosen to conduct his dealings with
the world in any part of its life we know outside the Bible.
"Without being so irreverent as to question God's *power*,"
the listener may say to himself, "is it right to suppose, in
the light of all that we know elsewhere, that this is how he
chooses to act?"

Answers to these questions will vary with the philosophical
stance and theological outlook of the interperter. If one bases
his interpretation on the literal factuality of the accounts,
however, he is obligated to do so with some better logic than
one recently published discussion which said:

After all, our magicians, our chemists, and our surgeons can do
even better things [than turn water to wine], and while the
amateur eye cannot keep up with them, we know there is a
logical explanation. Should we limit God to less than we allow

to men, especially when He had so good a reason to gladden the poor and to give Christ glory? [9]

The implied syllogism is unfortunate in its implications for faith: Magicians show us wonders in which the quickness of the hand deceives the eye; God must not be barred from wonders the magician can perform; therefore God must be allowed to produce faith by a great illusion. If the interpreter does not see these implications in his statements, he may be sure that others will.

When secular writers reason from the wonder-working power of science to conclusions concerning faith, religious leaders are quick to brand such thinking as "scientism" and to disavow the pertinence of physical wonders in the spiritual realm. They should then be equally sensitive to an inversion of scientism in which they argue from spiritual source to physical wonder—and even more wary of the religious application of scientism which supposes that physical wonders are an authentication of spiritual reality. Those whose faith is vital and secure are not dependent on such supports, for they have a faith rooted in personal decision about and experience with their Lord. To base faith on anything less is to make it insecure and superficial. Whatever be our position with regard to the miraculous element in the Scriptures, we ought to make it clear that saving faith does not rest upon it.

In all that matters most, the Bible is characterized by dependable order. God keeps covenant. His love is not subject to changing impulse or whimsy. His moral order is undeviating and undeceived. His providential care is trust-

[9] *The Miracles of Christ,* by David A. Redding (Westwood, N.J.: Fleming H. Revell Company, 1964), p. 8.

worthy. He numbers the hairs of our heads and marks the sparrow's fall. Even in its observations of the natural world, the Bible notes the impressive regularities of the seasons: night and day, the movements of the heavenly bodies, the fruitfulness of the earth—"first the blade, then the air, then the full grain in the ear" (Mark 4:28). The interpreter will speak most convincingly to the contemporary mind, and will be truest to the Scripture, when he gives due weight to this aspect of biblical truth.

The mark of authentic miracle is not its capacity to produce astonishment but its ability to reveal truth that takes us beyond ourselves. The wonders of electronics and space probes are not properly miracles: they astonish until explanation or sheer repetition has made them commonplace; they do not reveal truth that takes us out of ourselves and our preoccupations. Biblical miracles, on the other hand, whether or not they astonish by the overpowering wonder of physical event, have a capacity to convey truth that takes us beyond ourselves. They need not destroy the basis of orderly life in revealing God to us. Indeed, as Paul Tillich observed, if we understand them so, "the manifestation of the ground of being would destroy the structure of being; God would be split within himself, as religious dualism has asserted." [10] In miracle there is (a) an event that excites wonder, (b) some response in recognition of God's act as having a relation to our lives, and (c) an acceptance of it as a sign-event which lifts us above and beyond ourselves.

The important question is not, "Did it happen literally as

[10] *Systematic Theology,* I (Chicago: University of Chicago Press, 1951), 116. This paragraph of my discussion draws heavily on Tillich's treatment of the subject, pp. 111-17.

the narrative portrays it?" but, "What does it mean concerning our Lord and our relation to his intention for us?" Yet it is pointless to ask the *meaning* of an event while we remain confused as to how to take what is being told us regarding the event itself. The essence of interpretation is that "a creative past is brought into meaningful relation to a present in which, without such interpretation, the power of the past event is lost." [11] But the seriousness with which the mind accepts the interpretation is conditioned by the coherence with which it is able to view the creative past to which reference is made. How then shall we assess the miracle-event under interpretation? What attitude toward its factuality will best sustain its reception as sign-event which, in meaningful relation to our present situation, will interpret and direct our life? It is not to be supposed that the preacher must go through such reasonings whenever he deals with the miraculous. Yet his credibility as witness and interpreter will depend on the integrity with which he relates himself to such considerations.

No one answer to the questions we have raised can cover the whole range of the miraculous in the Bible. The healing miracles of the New Testament fall, even on modern ears, with a note of factual credibility; when they relate bodily healing to such therapeutic factors as forgiveness (Luke 5:17-26), they speak to us in ways so directly meaningful as to require little interpretation. The talking snake of Genesis 3 falls clearly within the category of truth communicated through theological myth, or what in an earlier chapter

---

[11] G. Ernest Wright, "History and Reality," in *The Old Testament and Christian Faith,* Bernhard W. Anderson, ed. (New York: Harper & Row, 1963), pp. 176-77.

we styled an always-and-everywhere story as distinguished from a once-upon-a-time story. It is easy to see in Jonah an Old Testament parable similar, both in its teaching purpose and its fictional composition, to our Lord's parables as recorded in the Gospels. Thus, from one type of narrative to another, the relation to a fact content may vary, while the capacity to point to truth regarding God's action in the world and its meaning in the interpretation of our lives remains constant.

How does the interpreter deal with such a difficult New Testament wonder story as that of the raising of Lazarus? Without appearing to assume its literal factuality, he may release the power of its message for listeners of this age. Some readers of the Johannine account may easily accept it as physical event, while others will be barred from serious consideration of any interpretation based on such a presupposition. Perhaps there is a way to deal with it which will estrange neither.

The story links new life with the Cross. Its one overshadowing affirmation is our Lord's declaration, "I am the resurrection and the life; he who believes in me, though he die, yet shall he live, and whoever lives and believes in me shall never die" (John 11:25-26). This is experienced fact which many of us have found true as new life has come to us in him, just as the Letter to the Ephesians sums it up: "You he made alive, when you were dead through the trespasses and sins in which you once walked" (2:1-2). Having found it so in known experience, we take these words with the assurance of faith when they are spoken beside the grave. But we know this new life is not cheaply bought, for the story of the raising of Lazarus closes with this dark note: "So from that day on they took counsel how to put him to death" (John 11:53). Here the link between the gift of new life and its cost on the Cross is recognized as unbreakable.

If the raising of Lazarus led directly to the Crucifixion, why is it nowhere mentioned in the other Gospels? Perhaps it is. The Gospel of John diverges from the Synoptic Gospels in its swift movement from event to meditation on the inner meaning. It lifts incidents out of the preaching of the apostles and interprets them. Is this what is happening in the account of Lazarus? The Gospel according to Luke has a Lazarus, too—the only character in all the parables of Jesus who has a name, and this a significant one, meaning "One whom God helps." In the parable both Lazarus and the rich man who neglected him at his gate died. In the place of torment the rich man begged to have Lazarus sent to warn his brothers still alive, that they might mend their ways. But he was told, "If they do not hear Moses and the prophets, neither will they be convinced if some one should rise from the dead" (Luke 16:31). Could John be working that out as it happened in the ministry of Jesus? When one rose from the dead they did not believe, but "from that day on they took counsel how to put him to death."

Men did rise from the dead, and this was the result. Zacchaeus was raised to new life, and religious men grumbled that Jesus had gone to dine with "publicans and sinners." A paralytic was given new life, and they asked, "Who is this that speaks blasphemies?" (Luke 5:21). A woman of the streets was given new life, and they said: "If this man were a prophet, he would have known who and what sort of

114

woman this is who is touching him, for she is a sinner" (Luke 7:39). From one kind of death or another he raised each of these, and in each instance it drove him nearer to the Cross.

Does this not picture his relation to us? "You he made alive, when you were dead through trespasses and sins in which you once walked"—that is our story. Zacchaeus and the rest hold the mirror to us. We live, but the price of our life is his cross. Eugene O'Neill has Lazarus say, "Laugh with me! Death is dead! Fear is no more! There is only life!" [12] In the O'Neill play a Roman general reports the power of the Christians to laugh at death, as he has seen them do in countless executions. He is dealing with sober fact. Stephen's sublime death surely had its part in the conversion of Saul of Tarsus; Paul's willingness to hazard death, again and again, won countless others and dotted churches all about the Mediterranean; "the blood of the martyrs was the seed of the church"; and in our own day the willing, almost debonair death of a Dr. Paul Carlson in the Congo stirs and moves a jaded world.

How can all these face death so? In the O'Neill play Tiberius sums up the findings of his investigation: "The miracle"—Tiberius credits Lazarus with having contrived it—"was done in conjunction with another Jew acting as this man's tool. This other Jew, the report states, could not possibly have possessed any magic power Himself, for Pilate crucified Him a short time after and He died in pain and weakness within a few hours. But this Lazarus laughs at

[12] *Lazarus Laughed,* Act I, scene 1. Copyrighted by Random House and reprinted by permission.

death!" [13] As well he might! For this "other Jew" had won the victory over it.

And well may we, for the victory is won for *us*. In dying, our Lord faced all the concentrated powers of evil and death. In raising him from the dead God defeated death and all the forces of the kingdom of evil. The victory won through his cross and resurrection opens the way to victory for every child of God. When, borrowing courage from his victory, and love from his love, we face life and death in this faith, we too can take up our crosses—even as he said we must— assured that they keep his gift of new life going forward in the world he has won. This strange power that links a cross to new life is still at work among us, in Martin Luther King, James Reeb, Dr. Tom Dooley, and many another. It is a gift to us. It can be a gift through us. But it comes always as God's gift in Christ, who will raise us from every death into which sin and evil betray us.

The interpreter often shuns difficult texts until, placed under orders by lectionary or Bible book course, he is faced unavoidably with a passage he would not have chosen for himself. Confronting such texts, he discovers aspects of the gospel which might otherwise have remained closed to him. The discipline makes more complete the nurture he supplies for his people's faith and, in his struggle to deal adequately with texts too big for him, his insight and powers of interpretation grow. In following an orderly plan which holds him to the steady facing of a wide expanse of biblical material, he need dread no monotony in his interpretation. For within the planned unity there is room for much variety in patterns. That potential falls to the next chapter to explore.

[13] *Ibid.*, Act III, scene 2.

For Further Study

1. The minister who has never submitted to the lectionary as a mentor in the choice of texts—and who consequently tends to look on such a discipline as forbidding—has a happy surprise awaiting him. Given some guidance as to what the lectionary and the Christian year are trying to do, and how to use them, such preaching can be exciting to the interpreter and helpful to the congregation. I have tried to give such guidance in *Living Doctrine in a Vital Pulpit,* which devotes one chapter to a basic correlation of the year with aspects of the *kerygma,* and follows with six chapters keyed to preaching on themes which highlight the respective major seasons. *Preaching the Christian Year,* edited by Howard Albert Johnson (New York: Charles Scribner's Sons, 1957), oriented to the more detailed Anglican calendar of the year, can be helpful to non-Anglicans as well.

The Bible book course supplies one of the most creative aspects of what is possibly the best of Andrew Blackwood's numerous meaty books on preaching, his *Preaching from the Bible* (Nashville: Abingdon Press, 1941). It is helpful not only to have expositions of the theory of such an approach to the preaching task, but to see how others have gone about it. Although Harold Bosley's method is not our suggested three months of consecutive sermons but a monthly sermon over a longer period from the chosen book, his *Sermons on the Psalms* and *Sermons on Genesis* (Apex eds.; Nashville: Abingdon Press, 1966 and 1964 respectively) offer strong examples of this kind of preaching. My own *Encounter with Christ* (Nashville: Abingdon Press, 1961) is the product of a three-month course, with three additional sermons, their sequence slightly rearranged for publication purposes.

2. Keeping a devotional diary might prove as creatively helpful to you as it has to many another. Its discipline in private worship is sufficient reason for undertaking it, but its added value in providing insights for subsequent book-course sermons makes it doubly a treasure. A notebook and Bible are all the equipment you need. The choice of a book for your initial venture and as the possible basis of a course a year hence—one of the Gospels would probably be best to start with—is all the preparation you require. Pages 99 ff. outline sufficient methodology. Today would be the best time to begin!

3. You need not wait until next year to try your hand at a book course. Andrew Blackwood's method (see his book listed above) is to spend three months studying a Bible book, followed immediately by three months of preaching from it. The longer preparation we have recommended has strong advantages, but Blackwood's method could help you get started. You might set aside two Bible periods in your daily schedule for this initial quarter, one for your devotional diary with a Gospel, and the other for more directly homiletic study of an epistle or a prophetic book. The Bible course is an approach to preaching so valuable as to justify no little effort to arrange and guard the time for making a proper beginning.

5

The Interpreter's Varied Patterns

FRESHNESS THROUGH VARIETY

The term "biblical preaching" can be deceptive as, textbook fashion, we classify types of sermons: topical, doctrinal, ethical, life situation—and biblical. Among these categories there is many an overlap. More important for our present consideration, "biblical preaching" is a catch-all phrase indicating a unified purpose to let the Word interpret and direct us, within which the varieties are all but limitless. A recently published book of strong biblical sermons delivered by the same preacher in a university chapel offers wide variety in type and method. There are expository treatments of Bible passages, topical developments of biblical ideas, Bible lectures, treatment of sentence texts, and existential approaches to human problems biblically considered by double analysis.[1]

This fact lends encouragement to the interpreter who projects an extended sequence of sermons rooted in biblical material. Moving on no dead level of monotony, such preaching can achieve the fascination of constant freshness within the stability of cumulative exposure to a solid body of biblical text. Within the year, or within the three-month course, there can be sermons which introduce or interpret a Bible book as a whole, vistas of life from the heights of towering chapters, interpretation through meaty paragraph pericopes, the incisiveness of sentence texts, the drama of Bible biographies —a colorful moving pageant.

To deal thus with the Bible is to guard against the evil of text mincing, into which even memorably strong preachers can fall. Note, for example, Edward Irving's "Preparation for Consulting the Oracles of God," preached early in the nineteenth century. Its strengths are notable. Its rounded periodic prose could win respect in the age of Carlyle and Ruskin. Though it uses its snippet of a text only as a motto to set at the beginning, its topical development takes manful issue with vices to which religious men of the time fell prey.

Forthrightly it warns against a kind of churchmanship which stresses doctrines that divide the body of Christ, identi-

---

[1] This refers specifically to *Encountering God,* by W. B. Blakemore (St. Louis: Bethany Press, 1965), which is particularly fertile in inventive use of varied approaches and methods; but in some sense the same could be said of other books of strong biblical preaching. On "double analysis" see pp. 20-26 and 78 above.

fying faith too exclusively with intellectual formulations. The Bible, Irving declares,

is hunted for arguments and texts of controversy, which are treasured up for future service. . . . The spirit of such readers becomes lean, being fed with abstract truths and formal propositions; their temper uncongenial, being ever disturbed with controversial suggestions; their prayers undevout recitals of their opinions; their discourse technical announcements of their faith. . . While the warm fancies of the Southerns [Irving speaks as a European] have given their idolatry to the ideal forms of noble art, let us Northerns beware we give not our idolatry to the cold and coarse abstractions of human intellect.[2]

Nobly said! Much in us still needs the rebuke.

Yet there is sad irony here. This sermon, intended to exalt the Scriptures, builds on a distortion of its own text! The phrase, "search the scriptures" (John 5:39), standing alone, has been wrenched from its context to make an imperative exhortation of what in its own setting was a kind of grudging admission of sorry fact. "You search the scriptures, because you think that in them you have eternal life, and it is they that bear witness to me; yet you refuse to come to me that you may have life." (John 5:39-40.) The full sentence would have led to a proclamation of Jesus Christ as Lord of the Scriptures and might have set the preacher's feet on even greater heights, as he portrayed the unity of the Bible held together in Christ. Instead, the piecemeal text was made an admonition bordering on bibliolatry, utterly devoid of the proclamation of Christ as Lord and Savior.

[2] *The World's Great Sermons,* Grenville Kleiser, ed. IV (New York: Funk and Wagnalls Company, 1908), 113-15.

The interpreter who deals with the lectionary in the light of an integrated biblical theology, or with the wholeness of Bible book courses, need not fall into this trap. Yet he need sacrifice nothing of timeliness, if he sees how the interpretation of any text leads to *its* interpretation of *us;* and nothing of change and inventiveness, if he keeps ever before him the rich variety of methods which comprise the unity of biblical preaching. We shall not attempt here to deal with these methods in the completeness of detail to be found in textbooks devoted exclusively to that task.[3] With only such guidance as will fill in the picture, we undertake the more modest task of observing how these varied patterns, taken together, can give rounded wholeness to the preaching sequences we have proposed.

THE BIBLE BOOK SERMON

We begin with the book sermon. Here the preacher undertakes, in a single address, to interpret our life through the book as a whole. He is encouraging his people to read it in its entirety, as they would any other book, looking for its total pattern. So doing, he builds bulwarks to defend against the error of regarding the Bible as an anthology of maxims, into which no small part of our customary use of the Scripture delivers us. The book was written to convey an overall message not always seen in considerations of its separate passages. In the book sermon the preacher sets himself to deliver that message.

Serving its own high ends, even when not associated with a book course, this type of sermon may come with peculiar

---

[3] See suggestions for further study appended to this chapter.

appropriateness at the beginning or end of a course. The preacher has been reading and rereading the book, familiarizing himself with its setting, analyzing its contents. As he and his people enter the course together, it will be helpful for the congregation to have some exposure to this background. Preaching such a sermon is not easy. It should speak for the book in its wholeness and unity, using enough of the book's own material to convey its drama and concreteness. Yet it must be selective, not trying to say everything, but majoring in the essential. Difficult as this is, it can lure the preacher by its worthy challenge and fascinate the listener by its new and revealing approach to the Scriptures.

Book sermons are of two kinds, one of which may more properly be called a Bible *lecture.* Its intent is to stimulate the hearer to read the book and to guide him to better understanding as he reads. It sets the book in the midst of the conflict in which it first played its part. For it is to be remembered that the Bible scene is always one of conflict, battle after battle in the general warfare of God against evil. There is an author to be introduced, a challenge to be understood, a purpose to be traced. Against this background the interpreter delivers the unfolding message of the book. Such a sermon on the first or second Sunday of a course can bring a vital contribution to the congregation.

The book *sermon,* more properly so labeled, addresses itself to the task which belongs to every sermon, its one difference being that its "text" is neither verse, nor paragraph, nor chapter, but nothing less than the entire book. Which is to say that such a sermon sets out to produce the encounter between these men and the Word to which the reading of the whole book gives rise. The Bible *lecture* is an *exposition* about the book; but the book *sermon* is meant to *execute* its message, to isolate some dark area of our experience and throw the light of the book upon it, to interpret our life in the perspective which the book provides. No more than the lecture can it say everything the book says, its mission and method being to detect the principal theme of the book—or one of its most important themes—and, using carefully selected material from the book's key passages, let that theme speak directly into our contemporary life. Useful in itself, such a sermon gains double value on one of the closing Sundays of a course, confronting the congregation with the total impact of what previously has been seen in its detailed episodes.

As such a sermon lets past proclamation become Word again, it brings together the most vital thing the book is saying and the most crucial need or denial our life hurls against it. From the encounter of the two it formulates the theme that puts us under examination. Here, for instance, is the Letter to the Colossians, challenging the philosophies with which men in its day were smothering Christian faith and making Christ only one more among the sources of such world views. That, says the preacher, thinking of many a sophisticated challenge in a so-called "post-Christian" age, is still going on. Preparing a book sermon highlighting the confrontation, he preaches on "Christ or Our Popular Gods." Or reading the Galatian Letter, hurled in the teeth of false notions of freedom, he feels himself in the very midst of a similar current confusion. So he preaches from this Epistle on the theme, "Emancipated—But Are We Free?" Again, reading I Peter's brave answer to undeserved suffering, and thinking of some of his flock whose anguish he carries in his heart, he sets out to open this resource for their support. Near the end of the letter, as he rereads it in the Moffatt translation, he comes upon the injunction, "Keep your foothold in the faith, and learn to pay the same tax of suffering as the rest of your brotherhood throughout the world" (5:9). Taking his cue from this, he uses the whole message of the book as he speaks of "When Suffering Collects Life's Tax."

In formulating themes the preacher is guided by principles which apply to sermons of all types: (a) A theme must be so stated as to be true to the message of the book—or other text—on which it is based. (b) It must talk about just one aspect of our life, brought to a burning focus. (c) It must have immediate significance, beamed at a real present need, perplexity, or denial. (d) It must major in the good news of God in Christ. (e) Its statement must convey some indication of action, of things vital going on—a verb, a contrast to be resolved, a tension to be brought to harmony, a fearful question to be answered.

These principles are not peculiar to the theme for a book sermon, though this type may present more than usual temptations to depart from them.

THE CHAPTER SERMON

The chapter sermon need not detain us long. Its teaching values are great, first because some of the structural insights of the Bible are distilled within chapters of massive import, and second because most Bible readers have favorite chapters to which they often return, so that new meanings evoked from such passages are reinforced again and again as the old loved path is retraced. An occasional sermon based on one

or another of the so-called "golden chapters of the Bible" can
be rewarding in itself and treasured by many persons in
the congregation. The preacher might even poll the congregation for their favorite chapters, compiling a list which
would lead eventually to a sermon series. Most of the major
books on which a course might be based present some moun-
tain-peak chapters; a sermon or two of this type could well
be included in the course.

It is not difficult to assemble a list of chapters on which
sermons could set forth the vital themes that interpret our
life. God's relation to his creation (Gen. 1) could begin it.
Our fallen and disrupted nature (Gen. 3) would immediately
come in view. The structure of ordered and responsible life
would stand forth in the Commandments (Exod. 20). Our
place within the great deliverance of God (Deut. 6) would be
celebrated. Our comfort in a dangerous world (Ps. 23)
would call for attention. The telescoping of the Exodus as
the experience of both a people and an individual (Ps. 66)
would find poetic interpretation. The sturdy and awesome
realities of worship (Isa. 6) would make themselves known.
The salvation won by God's Suffering Servant (Isa. 53)
would take its central place. God's new covenant with his
people (Jer. 31) would declare its promise of a better life.
Integrity would be revealed as the key to life (Micah 6).
The nature of life as crisis (Matt. 25) would be laid bare.
The victory of Calvary (Mark 15) would etch itself upon the
mind. The gospel in miniature would shine forth from the
chapter of the lost and found (Luke 15). The comfort of the
Christ of all times and places (John 14) would speak. Our
predicament and God's response (Rom. 7) would find succinct expression. The centrality of love (I Cor. 13) and

the power of the Resurrection (I Cor. 15) would be celebrated. Our call to be God's covenant people (I Peter 2) would be heard. And God's final victory in a new heaven and a new earth (Rev. 21) would come in view.

Such lists are not important. No "shorter Bible" so selected can be adequate. Lists will vary with their compilers. The above, however, may serve to suggest the possibilities of watershed chapters. The *method* of preaching on the chapter is not significantly different from that which applies to the book or paragraph, and need not be treated in detail here. Noting that a sermon or two of this type can set highlights in a Bible book course, we turn to other patterns.

THE PARAGRAPH SERMON

Consider the sermon based on a Bible paragraph or a passage of approximately paragraph length. Staple method, carrying the load of the majority of sermons in both the book course and the seasons of preaching from the lectionary, it presents four real advantages. (a) It is based on a text brief enough to reduce the problems of selectivity encountered in the chapter or book sermon. (b) It embodies a whole event or unit of thought possessing its own significance and unity. (c) It contains within itself sufficient amplitude of statement not only to set the theme but to guide the development of the sermon. (d) It returns to the original intention of the passage; for, as form criticism has shown, many pericopes, especially in the Gospels, are self-enclosed units having their origin as preaching material in the early church.

127

In most instances sermons on the parables belong to this category of preaching. Though there is far more to be said concerning the interpretation of Jesus' parables than can be attempted here, certain central matters identify their use with the principles governing paragraph preaching. (a) A parable says one thing and is nearly always distorted in meaning when allegorized or made to teach a variety of lessons. (b) Though the parables as we now have them in the Gospels are sometimes separated from their original contexts in the teaching of Jesus, it is generally important to take the context fully into account in interpreting the meaning. (c), The parables speak to such vital human concerns that they reveal their meaning most fully when set again in the living context of parallel needs in our own lives.

All this becomes concrete in Helmut Thielicke's sermon on "The Parable of the Mustard Seed" (Matt. 13:31-33). Since its literary context is simply that of Matthew's little book of collected parables, Thielicke sets it down in its probable life setting as Jesus told it. His hearers looked to his leadership with mingled expectancy and excitement. Describing them, Thielicke uses terms which identify them with our similar concerns.

It makes an ultimate difference whether a man looks at the strange enterprise of this Nazarene with the reserve of a sympathetic spectator—this costs nothing, and if the affair gets too hot he can always bail out in time—or whether he throws in his whole existence with this Jesus of Nazareth, whether, for example, he has given up his job and staked everything on this one card.[4]

[4] *The Waiting Father,* p. 61.

Those who first heard this parable, the sermon points out, had committed themselves to Jesus with this kind of finality. But, they were beginning to wonder, was it making any proportionate difference in the life of the world? Where was there any sign that the kingdom was coming?

To keep the bond firm between these men and our kind of life, Thielicke tells the story of the first Bible-study hour he conducted as a young pastor. He was trying to trust God as Lord of history in the midst of German life with Hitler in the saddle.

And in this Bible-study hour I was faced by two very old ladies and a still older organist. He was a very worthy man, but his fingers were palsied and this was embarrassingly apparent in his playing. . . . And outside marched the battalions of youth who were subject to altogether different lords. . . . If it really were nothing more than this—then isn't [Jesus] refuted by this utterly miserable response? [5]

Having thus set the problem that called forth the parable in conjunction with the problem as it confronts us now, Thielicke states the main contention of the sermon, which is the same as the one important thrust of the parable.

When Jesus speaks of the mysteries of growth he is not thinking so much of the quantitative process by which his church grows ever larger and finally, in a mighty Christian invasion, conquers the continents and islands, but rather of the fact that in his church there is an indwelling dynamic which must lay hold upon everything around it. [6]

[5] *Ibid.*, p. 62.
[6] *Ibid.*

129

He then develops this idea around three points drawn directly from the encounter of the parable with our life. First, we see this truth corroborated by looking at "the other images in which the church is portrayed as a dynamic force" in the teaching of Jesus. Second, this parable emphasizes not "external growth and bigness" but "the growth of a Christian's functioning, . . . of his maturing in his mission and effectiveness." Third, the parable "does not say that we as *Christians* or that we as the *church* are like a seed or leaven" but "the *kingdom of God* is both of these."

Whether the paragraph on which he proposes to preach contains a parable or some other kind of material, the interpreter arrives at its meaning by the same disciplined steps:

1. He studies the passage in its context, taking into account not only what comes immediately before and after it, but its larger context in the Scripture. What is its place in, and relation to, the total outline of the book of which it is a part? What does the main theme of the book suggest concerning the meaning of this paragraph? How does the good news of the victory of God's love over the kingdom of evil, won in Jesus Christ, speak to us through this paragraph?

2. Against this background he studies the passage itself to discover the one important truth which runs through it and is the reason for its existence.

3. He analyzes the structure of the passage in search of the component parts of its statement of this truth.

4. He puts our life under examination in the light of what the passage is saying. What does it require of those who accept its promise? How is our life at odds with it? What doubts or resistances do our practical affairs, if not our

130

words, fling back in its face? What liberation does it bring us when we are ready to meet its terms?

5. From this understanding of our life in the light of the passage he sets down in a few articulate words the purpose this indicates for the sermon.

6. He crystallizes the central idea of the sermon in a single declarative sentence. This is the proposition, which every section of the sermon must explain, amplify, or support.

He is then ready to develop the outline and write the sermon through which the text will interpret us, conveying God's Word to us in our situation.

THE BIOGRAPHICAL SERMON

An occasional sermon dealing with a Bible biography affords attractive possibilities of change of pace. In the modern sense of the term the Bible has no interest in biography. Historical details are not its business. History as conveyor of a message, however—*Heilsgeschichte*—binds it all together. In this process it speaks through the unfolding lives of persons. Here is gripping drama, which the pulpit can ill afford to pass unnoticed. Full of vivid action and human interest, it has rich possibilities of riveting attention, a necessary condition of communication. Luminous, it lights up what our lives mean and what God is seeking to do for and through us. Evoking our identification with characters in many ways like ourselves, it facilitates that appropriation of the history as *our history* through which revelation comes to us.

Little wonder that, in the hands of such a giant as George Matheson, biographical preaching still speaks to us across the gap of generations. Employed by lesser men today, it produces hours of insight whose effects for many a listener linger through the years. The biographical sermon does not require a Bible book course as context, but it can highlight any course; and almost every major book in either testament will provide material for at least one such sermon.

Two keys to vitality—in addition to faithful research and vivid storytelling—must be borne in mind. First of these is the remembrance of what is essential in all preaching but more easily forgotten in the narrative interest of biography: The sermon must deal, first and last, with some quandary or struggle *of which we are a part*. It is not a sermon about a figure in history, from which some lessons are drawn; it is a sermon about *our life in one of its dangerous and crucial aspects,* on which the experience of a known character throws light. It is not narrative, but *message which employs narrative as a means*. Its purpose is not mainly to interpret the historic person but to interpret our life through another whose encounter with God in the midst of his struggle illumines ours. It is not *exposition* of past proclamation but *execution* of the text as it becomes Word again in our facing of this figure and God's dealings with him.

In our enthusiasm for the character we easily lose this focus. A minister whose years of hobby study in the life of Abraham Lincoln produced Lincoln lectures packed with drama and urgency, was startled when his brother half-facetiously said: "I wish you could get as excited about the Lord Jesus Christ as you do about Abraham Lincoln." No discourse is valid preaching which forgets that, and no preaching is more exposed to the danger of displaced focus than the biographical sermon.

Suppose the minister were to preach on the pilgrimage through which Jacob became Israel. He might bring the material on this figure, scattered through many chapters of Genesis, within manageable frame by taking his stand at the climactic moment of change in the wrestle by the brook Jabbok (Gen. 32:24-31). All that goes before and all that follows flows like sand in an hourglass through the narrow neck of this episode. In this moment we have the key to what all the rest means. To *tell the story* from the standpoint of this night of crisis, however, is not enough. Such narration may produce a strong biographical *lecture* but will fall short of becoming a vital *sermon*. Where, the preacher must ask, is the crucial point of *encounter with our life*?

He may conclude that it lies in our problem of how to get ourselves off our hands. These obtrusive selves so get in our way that we keep stumbling over them. If we try to get rid of them by losing ourselves in some "interest" or good work, that takes us only a little way and lets us down. We keep examining ourselves to see if the trick is working, pulling up the seeds of the new life to see if they are sprouting. There is a deeper question: How can we become men and women God can use? What strange mixtures we are! Tender within the family circle, ruthless in our dealings outside. Faithful to duty and spoiling it all with some passionate outburst or unforgiving bitterness toward those who do not measure up to our standards. How do we get these selves off our hands? How do we become people God can use?

See how it happened with Jacob. Here the preacher may trace the problem as it darkened Jacob's years. But see, he says, how Jacob became a man God could so use that for all time his name is linked with the divine name. To this day one of the names by which the God of the Bible is known is "the God of Abraham, and Isaac, and Jacob." How do such men

133

as we are and Jacob was come to this change? Here by the ford of the Jabbok we find the way.

It comes, first, through struggle that does not run away from the issue that torments us, but wrestles through to a conclusion. The preacher may note that this story, probably based on an old legend dealing with a river god, has its ambiguities, never coming down quite flat-footed as to whether Jacob wrestled with a man (that buried other self we cannot escape?) or an angel (a messenger of God—could that be conscience?) or God himself. Perhaps that is because life is ambiguous, never clearly labeling which of these we encounter in our wrestles. Suffice it that Jacob did not shirk the struggle. What about us?

It comes, second, through surrender that leaves a proud man limping (note vss. 25 and 31). When life harrows us up, is it getting ready to make something of us? Proud and self-sufficient, we have ourselves on our hands; limping, wounded, with the mark of the Cross upon us, we may begin to count for God. Who of us is without wounds? But are they the wounds of the Cross?

It comes, finally, through repentance that means an entire change of outlook. Not a little tinkering, a few improvements, another resolution, but a change that goes deep. Jacob's change was so sweeping as to call for a new name to fit the new man. Are we trying to make do with the old one?

Whenever he deals with a Bible biography the preacher will first bend his efforts to find how it speaks currently to his people's need.

A second key to vitality in preaching of this genre lies in the recognition that the biographical sermon must show some progression in the life of the figure studied, by tapping its events at two or more points in time. The examination of a single incident is static—a still projection of one frame in what should be a moving picture. As we have seen with Jacob, a single episode may be used as the dramatic highlight, the key to the meaning of the rest. If this device is used, however, there must be flashbacks and forward movement. God is *doing something* with this man—or the devil is taking him—and we cannot see *our* lives in his mirror unless the image moves, as we must.

Stopping the action for replay at three points on the time scale of Demas' life lends power to the sermon Harry Emerson Fosdick based on that obscure New Testament personality. The opening paragraph of this memorable New Year's sermon on "The Power to See It Through" shows the pattern to which the whole idea is cut:

Concerning one character in the New Testament, mentioned only three times, one suspects that many Christians have not even heard—Demas. He illustrates one of the most familiar tragedies in human life—a fine beginning and a poor ending. He lacked the power to see it through. First, in Paul's letter to Philemon, we read, "Demas, Luke, my fellow-workers." So Demas, along with Luke, and named first at that, was standing by Paul in his Roman imprisonment, a devoted and promising disciple. Second, in Paul's letter to the Colossians, we read, "Luke, the beloved physician, and Demas." Reading that, one wonders why Demas and Luke, who were praised together at the first, were separated in this passage as though Luke indeed retained Paul's confidence as "the beloved physician" but Demas had become merely "Demas." Third, in the second letter to Timothy, incorporating, we suppose, one of the last messages Paul ever wrote, we read,

"Demas forsook me, having loved this persent age." Three points on a curve, that enable us to plot its graph! For here is the story of a man who made an excellent beginning and a wretched ending; Demas, my fellow-worker; Demas; Demas forsook me.[7]

Numerous possibilities for the illumination of our lives from other characters by this device will occur to the interpreter. See, for instance, what happens if Mark is caught at three crucial moments. In Acts 15:38 we read of him as "one who had withdrawn from them in Pamphylia, and had not gone with them to the work." Why he had given this unpromising account of himself in the face of danger and great opportunity we do not know, but there his desertion stands with its sorry blot on the record. But Acts 15:39 continues: "Barnabas took Mark with him and sailed away to Cyprus." Paul and Barnabas had clashed over the issue, Paul insisting that in this foray into the wild hazards of pagan territory there was no place for a teammate who had proved so poor a risk. Barnabas, with his genius for giving doubtful characters another chance (Had he not been the one who vouched for Paul himself in a church that knew only the persecutor Saul?)—Barnabas stood by Mark even to the parting of the ways. He "took Mark and sailed." Finally, in II Timothy 4:11 we hear the upshot of the matter. Paul writes from prison, lonely, sick, cold, and needing a strong friend, "Get Mark and bring him with you; for he is very useful in serving me." Mark "who had withdrawn from them"; "Barnabas took Mark and sailed"; "Get Mark and bring him . . . , for he is very useful." Under God that can happen, even after sorry blots have stained our record.

[7] (New York: Harper & Brothers, 1935), p. 1.

GUIDELINES TO TEXTUAL INTERPRETATION

The sentence text is by so much the commonest type of scriptural base for a sermon that it calls for little special attention here. From every book on which a course might conceivably be preached sentences of singular importance cry for attention in sermons that will bring out the encounter with the Word to which they lead. Most books speak through some sentences full of heart warmth, offering foundations for memorable sermons. In every book, but more especially in the Gospels, where the pithy sayings of Jesus play the role, there are sentences which carry heavy cargoes of meaning gathered up from the whole incident or passage of which they are a part.

The short text, gathering wide suggestiveness into narrow compass, is a rhetorical instrument so powerful that it will be used; all the more important, therefore, that it be used well. What sort of study will enable the minister to use a text with accuracy as well as creative power, so that "in dealings with the text *its* being interpreted by us turns into *our* being interpreted by the text"? [8] Study of a text is not significantly different whether the passage to be dealt with is sentence, paragraph, or chapter. The same guidelines need to be followed in each case, but the shorter the text the more crucial the study which draws integrity of meaning from a larger context.

First, then, the interpreter must see the text in its setting. If he comes to this sermon as one step in a Bible book course, the very nature of that enterprise will contribute to this end. In any case, he must see the text against a background of

[8] See chapter 1, note 11.

historical reality. What does it say, not only in itself but as conditioned by its larger context? Where and when was it said, and what light do these surrounding conditions shed on its relation to the world of events? How did its challenge or promise affect men in its day? How does it relate itself to *us?* Why was it written: what was going on, what brought it forth? Who said it, and to whom? How does this affect our understanding of its meaning? The answers to these questions will begin to unlock its secrets.

Second, the interpreter must study the passage for its central meaning. If he has facility with the biblical languages he will read it in its own tongue. At any rate, he will read it in several different translations, which will go far toward freeing him from attaching undue weight to words or phrasing not essential to the meaning but hardly more than accidents of English idiom. He will consider it in the light of the *literary type* to which it belongs. Is it parable? Then he must look for the one central meaning, ignoring everything merely incidental to the story form. Is it poetry? Then he must pierce through the literary images to the meaning they symbolize. Is it apocalyptic? Then he must not linger over its lurid details but alert himself to what it says about the actions of the God of history in the crises of time. He will press the *words and grammatical structures* of the passage to yield up their truth. Only when he has thus worked with his own manful persistence—but not failing to do so then— he will check his findings by the best commentaries, Bible dictionaries, and word books to which he has access. All this search for central meaning he will finally distil in a paraphrase of the passage, which tells its truth in his own best words.

Third, the interpreter must listen to the passage for its personal import. How, he will ask, does it enter the dialogue of God with men? How does it speak to me now? For this purpose the self-searching and the listing of the troubled situations of other men whom he has encountered in his pastoral rounds will be useful.[9] Is the divine-human encounter as seen in this passage, developed further at other points in the Bible? How does that amplify the understanding of this text?

Finally, the interpreter must examine the passage as to its inner dynamics. What issue is joined? he will ask. What tensions develop within it? What movement is here? What is afoot, and where does it lead? What are the steps in the unfolding of its idea? When, for example, he deals with Luke 5:1-11 he will see beyond the historical record of the calling of Simon Peter to the more universal issue: the Lord Christ is beginning the making of a new man. The evangelist writing this into the Gospel is not so much concerned to fill in our knowledge about a man named Peter in the first century as to tell us something about how Christ comes into any man's life and what difference it makes. Three steps stand out in this encounter.

First, Jesus got Simon's boat. "Getting into one of the boats, which was Simon's, he asked him to put out a little from the land." (Vs. 3.) With the boat he got Simon's interest. Simon *heard* the teaching that day, in a way he might have missed if he had not been *involved*. Everything else that happened to Simon might have been blocked, finished, written off, never entered in the record, if he had refused the boat.

[9] On this useful discipline see chapter 1, p. 21.

What God does with us may begin with small things, but it does not stop with them.

Getting Simon's boat, Jesus asked for a hand in his business. "Put out into the deep and let down your nets for a catch." (Vs. 4.) Our Lord is never content with marginal issues. Sunday is not enough; he asks control from Monday through Saturday. Simon almost refused him: "Master, we toiled all night and took nothing!" You hear it in his tone: "Master, you're a good teacher, but *I'm* the *fisherman* here. You take care of the rabbi business, and I'll manage the fishing business. You don't know what I've been through in this trade, and how can you know its issues?" So near did Simon come to missing any further unfolding of his life with Jesus. Just in time, he managed to stammer his saving "Nevertheless."

Having got Simon's boat and his business, Jesus was not content until he got Simon. "And when they had brought their boats to land, they left everything and followed him." (Vs. 11.) Before that happened, of course, Simon got such an overpowering look at himself that he exclaimed, "Depart from me, for I am a sinful man, O Lord" (vs. 8). As if his Lord didn't know! Or as if that would keep Jesus from dealing with him, making something of him he had not dreamed possible! "Do not be afraid," said Jesus; "henceforth you will be catching men" (vs. 10). So Simon saw a new meaning and purpose in his life and gave a new allegiance. He left everything and followed. Of course he was not suddenly the man God meant him to become—that would come only at the end of a long road—but he was on his way.

Seeing the meaning of the passage, alive with its inner dynamics, the interpreter will brood over it, allow it to gather material about itself by the association of ideas, and finally outline and develop a sermon from it.

Biblical preaching possesses a powerful unity. It is always at work on the one great priority: bringing men into the encounter with the Word which puts their life in question, yet opens it to measureless possibilities. God reaches them through the text which becomes Word again, showing them who they are and who they can become. Always one, it is fascinatingly many-sided—carrying the powerful impact of a whole book of the Bible on one occasion, mounting to the heights of one of the Bible's watershed chapters on another, again laying bare the import of a paragraph into which the gospel is compressed, or seeing life's meaning in the shared experience of a pivotal character, or cutting to the heart of great matters with the incisiveness of a sentence text.

In all this, though we *use* important methodology, it is not *methods* that are at stake. We are not technicians, but interpreters. Here in the congregation are men and women fighting hard battles with increasing fearfulness that their resources will not hold out. They struggle to find their way to a decent and finally useful life in a day when the landmarks are misplaced and they are no longer sure which way to turn. Sick in body, they are even more ill with inner dread and gnawing guilt. They are crushed by the misused power of employers, or loved ones, or the sheer weight of mass society. They struggle to remake their life by the grim determination of their resolutions and cannot because the resolving will is itself infected with self-centeredness and sin. They try, with such lightheartedness as they can muster, to live as serenely as if life were theirs under permanent title; but there is the stark fact that, before another Sunday comes, the places of some will be vacant nevermore to be filled in this world.

Methods and texts are insufficient for such issues. We need a unified, comprehensive, saving gospel. We need a sense not of so many weekly *messages* to deliver but of *a message* that spans the Scriptures and runs its binding cable through our ministry. We need to hear in the varied and often baffling texts the abiding Word of the gospel. As we search for this integrating Word, two questions press for answer. How can we use the *whole* Bible, Old Testament as well as New, to give maximum effectiveness to a message which was fully spoken only *after* the Old Testament was completely written? How can we find our way all about the Scriptures, amazing in their differences of presentation, with a sure ability to find the abiding "gospel" in every text? In the two chapters that remain we shall seek light on these essential quests.

For Further Study

1. Various textbooks devoted exclusively to that task set forth the details of the homiletic principles reviewed in this chapter. *A Guide to Biblical Preaching,* by Chalmer Faw (Nashville: Broadman Press, 1962), gives a useful chapter to directions for each of the sermon types. Dwight E. Stevenson has contributed two valuable workbooks for the Bible book sermon: *Preaching on the Books of the New Testament* and *Preaching on the Books of the Old Testament* (New York: Harper & Row, 1956 and 1961 respectively). On methods of exegetical study of texts, *The Way to Biblical Preaching,* by Donald Miller (Nashville: Abingdon Press,

142

1957) is a compact, incisive handbook. *Proclaiming the Word,* by Ronald Sleeth (Nashville: Abingdon Press, 1964) further pursues the variety-in-unity of biblical preaching.

2. Have you begun the spadework for a Bible book course? If so, you will want to be alert to possibilities opened by all these types. Since the paragraph supplies the basic unit of study in your devotional diary, or the steps in your outline of the book in any analytic study, you need no special device to open the way to paragraph sermons. But you might well set aside a section of your notebook for references to one or two leading characters of the book you are studying, with notations concerning the facts given about them, and your reflections thereon. Another section might begin some study of one or two of the highly significant chapters. Still another might begin to list and scrutinize key sentences that could be used creatively as texts.

3. While you are at work on this long-range preparation, you can be taking some immediate forward steps in your preaching. If you have not found the joy of the paragraph sermon, you could begin to get experience with it. Should you need help getting started, you might make your own approach to a sermon from the nucleus offered on pp. 141-42. Better still, why not use one of the lessons from your church's lectionary for an approaching Sunday as the base for a paragraph development?

6

Christian Dialogue with the Old Testament

How Preach from Pre-Christian Sources?

Special questions confront the interperter as he turns to the Old Testament. In what sense does its text become God's Word, interpreting our life? "Christian preaching can find no ground in the Old Testament," say some thoughtful men, sensitive to the theological climate of today. "For the Old Testament has no Christ," they continue. "Its voice is the voice of law. Within its pages grace is seen dimly, if at all. Where love is present, it is not the love known in the New Testament."

The difficulty is not less for being old. Early in its pil-

144

grimage—in the teaching of Marcion, who set the Jewish scriptures over against the revelation in Christ—the church faced this problem. For Marcion the contrast Paul had drawn between law and gospel, flesh and spirit, the former age and the new age, led to a sharp break between the testaments. The God of the Old Testament, Marcion declared, was at variance with the God of the New. Labeled heresy by the church, rejected in Christian teaching, this point of view keeps creeping back to trouble us.

Its overtones are heard in the "Manifesto" issued by an influential theologian of the last generation at a crisis point in his creative career. He wrote of a change of some kind taking place in God. The event of the Cross, as he saw it, was so radical that the difference it effects in our status roots in "a change that has taken place *within God,* which makes possible also a change in his attitude toward men, a change in how he regards them, a change in what he is able to do for them." After the event of Calvary, God himself is different, for he has "admitted into his being an alien element" which requires his "undergoing structural reorganization." "The God of the Christian bears a scar" which formerly "was not actually there." "The cost of man's redemption is the dislocation of the normal internal structure of Deity." [1] For many a man the impact of such teaching drives the difference between the testaments as deep as a revolution in God himself. In such a theological climate, how are we to encounter in the Old Testament a word which interprets us who live in the shadow of the Cross and the light from the open tomb?

[1] Edwin Lewis, *A Christian Manifesto* (Nashville: Abingdon Press, 1934), pp. 169-70.

One answer, implicit in widespread practice, when not openly stated, has been to turn to the Old Testament as a source of moralistic exhortation, but to reserve proclamation of specifically Christian gospel for the preaching based on New Testament texts. "But is this adequate?" many a man has asked. "Ought not the clear note of the gospel to run through *all* our preaching? How can an honest treatment of the Old Testament render this possible?"

At another extreme the Old Testament has become a repository from which men mined "types" of Christ. "Everywhere the Scripture is about Christ alone" [2]—a position defensible by sophisticated definition of its terms—has often resulted in forced efforts to press from every passage a "type" of Christ and to see little else in the Old Testament. But this raises the question of honesty once more. Does a straightforward reading of the Old Testament documents support this as their own intent? Are we not under obligation to allow them to speak with their own peculiar voice? Must we not maintain intellectual integrity in dealing with our sources? If we coerce them to say what they did not originally intend, do we read them as *Scripture?* Have they not become mere echoes of what, on other grounds, we wish to find? But if the material did not originally convey the gospel in this sense, how are we to preach Christian gospel from it?

There is no escape from the experience of the centuries: that the Old Testament does interpret our life, and that it does so in ways which reinforce the good news of God as it comes to us in Jesus Christ. When it tells us of the Fall, we

---

[2] The title which Wilhelm Vischer borrowed from a phrase of Luther's for his essay in *The Old Testament and Christian Faith,* Anderson, ed., pp. 90-101.

know that this is a true picture of ourselves. Confronted by the divisions born of pride, at Babel we are constrained to say, "This is who we are." In a thoughtful reading of the Exodus we see the story of our captivity and deliverance and say, with men of Israel to this day, "This is 'what the Lord did for me when I came out of Egypt' " (Exod. 13:8). When God, of his own free choice, calls a people to be his servants, we hear his gracious call to us. With Hosea we see that the love which redeemed the unfaithful Gomer is no human creation; it comes from him who is the Source of all things and who loves us in our unfaithful ways. When the prophets address Israel, there is that in our conscience which makes us know the word is for us. When we open ourselves to it, we cannot doubt that the Old Testament interprets our life.

Yet the difficulty of dialogue with pre-Christian sources, which finds in them Christian gospel without doing violence to their integrity or ours, is sufficiently obvious to impel us to special study of the problem. We have seen from the beginning of these chapters that the task of preaching is not the mere *exposition* of historic texts, but such *execution* of them that past proclamation becomes present Word of God to us. When the past proclamation is pre-Christian, and our call is to proclaim Christ, what does that mean for our preaching?

CHRISTIANS FIND THEMSELVES INTERPRETED

The solution of the problem begins with an exploration of the *empirical reality* that when we read the Old Testament as Christians, it interprets our life. We cannot pretend otherwise than that through Jesus Christ we have met God in a way utterly normative for all other experience; yet into this experience the Old Testament speaks in ways without which we should be sadly impoverished.

In its native language of symbol the New Testament distils this truth in the Transfiguration story (Matt. 17:1-8). Peter's proposal of three booths, for Moses, Elijah, and Jesus, was rejected, not by Jesus, but by a voice from the cloud—that is to say, by God himself. "This is my beloved Son, with whom I am well pleased," said the voice; "listen to him" (vs. 5). As the scene closed, "they saw no one but Jesus only" (vs. 8). That is: in the temple of Christian faith and experience there is not room for three niches, setting Moses, Elijah, and Jesus—the law, the prohpets, and the Christ—on one level. We hear One above all others. In a way none can share we see Jesus only. Yet we understand him better as we see him in conversation with Moses and Elijah, who, as Luke observes, "spoke of his departure, which he was to accomplish at Jerusalem" (9:31). His departure—his "exodus"—is thus associated with the great deliverance which stands dominant in the Old Testament, and through this image we see with a new richness the Christ who delivers us from sin and death. His ultimate struggle wins the battle which occupies both testaments. The preacher interprets this truth, not by forcing fanciful typology on the Old Testament but by penetrating

to the real event about which the Old Testament bears witness; an event that belongs to our own lives. The Old Testament is a history of *humanity's* liberation, humanity's conflict, in the destiny of a single people, a conflict to get free of sin, a conflict that is won in Christ's death and resurrection. In my present life the same conflict is taking place, because I am a man and belong to the humanity whose struggle goes on in Israel.[3]

Our Trinitarian experience of God goes with us as we read the Old Testament. There we meet God as Creator, Lawgiver, Lord of history. But he is more. He is the Father of our Lord Jesus Christ. Unhesitatingly the New Testament writers so identify him, as when the Letter to the Hebrews begins: "In many and various ways God spoke of old to our fathers by the prophets; but in these last days he has spoken to us by a Son" (1:1-2). Our experience of God in Christ controls all else—"God was in Christ reconciling the world to himself" (II Cor. 5:19)—yet we could not have recognized that it was *God* we were meeting if we had had no knowledge of him before. He who spoke in the Old Testament "by the prophets" was the Father of our Lord.

As, in typical New Testament experience, he is interpreted by the Holy Spirit, so the Spirit interprets him in the Old. "The Lord God has sent me and his Spirit," Deutero-Isaiah announces (48:16).

> The Spirit of the Lord God is upon me,
> because the Lord has anointed me
> to bring good tidings to the afflicted

declares Trito-Isaiah (61:1). "The Spirit of the Lord fell upon me, and he said to me, 'Say, Thus says the Lord' "—so Ezekiel begins his message (11:5). And so it runs in passage after passage. It would be false to foist upon the Old Testament a developed doctrine of the Trinity; but it is manifestly true that, reading the Old Testament as men who cannot say

[3] Wingren, *The Living Word,* p. 49.

what we mean by God until we have said "Father," "Son," "Spirit," we are utterly at home.

In both testaments we meet the same God, holding an unbroken purpose in history. There is

an organic, dynamic unity which draws very simply from the fact that God always means the same thing. It is a unity which cannot be discerned in mere resemblances, or in coincidences of event, or in function, or in language. It is to be discerned in the deep and underlying patterns of "salvation history": Fall, Exodus, Judgment, Mercy, Sacrifice, Atonement. The very listing of these dominant motifs—and the list could be almost unbelievably drawn out: Fatherhood, Kingship, Messiahship, the People of God, Repentance, Forgiveness—the very listing of them should be in itself not only evidence enough that there can be no profound understanding of the New Testament apart from the Old, or of the Old apart from the New, but also warning enough that the difference between the two may never be reduced simply to contrast.[4]

Yet we dare not presume upon this unity. Before any Old Testament text can speak truly to us it must be allowed to put the truth on its own terms. Any undue haste to make it preach the gospel on our terms will destroy its message. Typology which nervously shuffles the pages for "foreshadowings of Christ" almost inevitably falls into this error. If we are to have typology, let it be of the sort which, not distorting the plain sense of the passage, patiently hears it out in its own voice before noting the overtones with which it vibrates for the ear attuned to the New Testament. Such a passage, for instance, as Genesis 22:1-18—Abraham's readiness to

[4] Scherer, *The Word God Sent,* pp. 39-40.

sacrifice Isaac—is best approached in this way, which allows it to become the Word of God speaking of both obedience and grace.

Taking his stand here, the preacher speaks of the saving relation of love between God and man, noting for the purpose a compound text which gathers up the elements of the passage. To Abraham's assured word that "God will provide himself the lamb for a burnt offering" (vs. 8), God responds: "Because you . . . have not withheld your son, your only son, I will indeed bless you, . . . and by your descendants shall all the nations of the earth bless themselves" (vss. 16-18). Sketching a swift picture of our lostness, the preacher asks, What can save our lost world? Love can! We know by heart the haunting words that tell how "God so loved the world that he gave his only Son" (John 3:16), but far back in the dawn of history there is the story of another father and another only son; and that, too, has something to say on the subject. Whether you read it in John 3:16, or in Genesis 22, it says one thing: God's love, evoking answering love from men, produces the saving relationship for a lost world.

God's love calls for an end of human sacrifice. The writer of this story in Genesis may well have been basing his narrative on an older tale of child offerings. For generations God sent his prophets to raise their cry against the practice. Here the preacher may fill in some of the Old Testament detail to document the prophetic protest (e.g., Micah 6:7; Deut. 18:10; Ps. 103:13). Finally a writer whose work is gathered up in Genesis may have presented this matchless story as a parable to show that God had no use for such sacrifices; he could himself provide the lamb. Does he not still rebuke us, who sacrifice children by the denial of human rights, the

151

perpetuation of ghettos and slums, the terrors of war, and our unrelenting drive for "success" which loads on young shoulders the burden of expectations they cannot bear? In its deep theological rooting of the protest against human sacrifice —heard here in God's own cry, "Do not lay your hand on the lad" (vs. 12)—this story calls to us in the name of a love that would have done with all that.

But God's love does more: it inspires an obedience based on love. Abraham was called to a terrible choice—between his love of God and his love of Isaac. Yet he could not be true to Isaac if he was false to God; just as we can give our children nothing worth having if we do not first give them a heritage of integrity. Abraham saw, as we must, that obedience came first—even for Isaac's sake. In the end obedience won, for it rested on love: his love for God and his love for Isaac. At the very last moment the conflict was resolved on a higher level, as he saw that his love was only derivative, a mere shadow cast by God's far greater love. God wanted no sacrifice of Isaac; he would provide himself the lamb. We who live on this side of Calvary can see it even more easily than Abraham could, but at all times God himself is love. We obey because his love has won us and we love.

So God's love embraces the world in blessing. In this story he blessed Abraham and promised to bless "all the nations of the earth" through him. God loves "all the nations." As John was to say later, he "so loved the *world*"— not a select few, not those who earned his love (Who ever *earned love*?), not just the righteous, not the church. "Your son, your only son," says the story in a line twice repeated. "Because you . . . have not withheld your son, your only son"

152

—what is the consequence? The blessing of the righteous Abraham? Yes, that; but beyond that, the most illogical thing: "all the nations of the earth shall bless themselves." Or is this the highest logic, love's logic—an overflow which cannot be stopped anywhere, but reaches to the most surprisingly far places? God knew about that. He, too, had an only Son; and he, too, loved. That love, accepted, can unchain our tensions and guilt, to move out and embrace a lost world.

Far better than a unity extracted from the Bible by the sleight of hand of fancied "foreshadowings," the unity that is present in the undeviating purpose of God, which speaks in the story itself, can confront us with the Word that interprets our life. As Christians, we read the *New* Testament, from beginning to end, in the light of one pivotal event, the Cross-Resurrection. In the New Testament we need no typology, no foreshadowing of the Cross; it is simply a part of God's love at every turn of the road. In like manner, as we read the Old Testament, we stand on the same ground made dear by faith, and see the same God at work. When the witnesses who knew him before Christ came have been allowed to speak in their own tone, we catch insights we would surely have missed in any haste to make them talk like Christians; but having heard them, we Christians better understand our Lord.

LAW ADDRESSES THE CHRISTIAN CONSCIENCE

In preaching Christian gospel from the Old Testament, a further aid is to be found in the truth that when we read these documents as men of conscience, for whom *law is*

153

structural to life, they speak to us with power. As the Articles of Religion of the English Reformation put it,

Although the Law given from God by Moses, as touching Ceremonies and Rites, do not bind Christian men, nor the Civil precepts thereof ought of necessity to be received in any commonwealth; yet notwithstanding, no Christian man whatsover is free from the obedience of the Commandments which are called Moral.[5]

Their claim upon us rests not on legalistic considerations, but on their sheer weight as matching the necessities of our life. Changing times may alter their enforcement of custom and culture, but the basic relations they enunciate remain inescapable as long as we are men.

So said Paul when his dichotomy of law and grace led to the question, "Are we to continue in sin that grace may abound?" Hear his emphatic "By no means" (Rom. 6:1-2); the claim upon us is essential to our life. "What return did you get from the things of which you are now ashamed? The end of those things is death." (Rom. 6:21.)

Law interprets us and gives meaning to our life. Is not this the force of such a declaration as that of Joshua 1:8? "This book of the law shall not depart out of your mouth, but you shall meditate on it day and night, that you may be careful to do according to all that is written in it; for then you shall make your way prosperous, and then you shall have good success." This is who you are, it seems to say, a creature whose life gets its very substance from a Word addressed to

[5] Article VII, as found in *The Book of Common Prayer,* or in John Wesley's abridgment Article VI.

154

it. You live by obedience. "Prosperity" and "success" in any fully human sense of the terms come to you as, hearing the claim of law, you *become* who you *are*. Within this covenant relation to God you find yourself—never so fully yourself as when most faithfully obedient to him.

Jesus, as bringer of the new covenant, declared with emphasis that it did not diminish the claim of the old. "Think not that I have come to abolish the law and the prophets," he said;

I have come not to abolish them but to fulfil them. For truly, I say to you, till heaven and earth pass away, not an iota, not a dot, will pass from the law until all is accomplished. Whoever then relaxes one of the least of these commandments and teaches men so, shall be called least in the kingdom of heaven; but he who does them and teaches them shall be called great in the kingdom of heaven (Matt. 5:17-20).

This stress runs through the Gospels. In what John sets forth as the first of Jesus' signs, at Cana of Galilee, he carefully notes that the six stone jars which Jesus ordered filled to the brim were "for the Jewish rites of purification" (2:6), as if to point the significance of the sign: that when Christ fills the receptacle of the law to the brim, what is drawn forth is something qualitatively and wonderfully new. Thus John weaves his spell of wonder around the straightforward synoptic declaration: "Therefore every scribe who has been trained for the kingdom of heaven is like a householder who brings out of his treasure what is new and what is old" (Matt. 13:52). The new spirit does not abrogate the old law.

All this makes clear that it is less than Christian gospel to

155

preach grace divorced from the context of law. To say that we are not to preach law in the legalistic spirit of the scribes and Pharisees is not to say that we are absolved from responsibility to preach it at all. "I don't think it is Christian to want to get to the New Testament too soon and too directly," wrote Dietrich Bonhoeffer in one of his letters from prison. In the same passage he confessed that he had been living much in the Old Testament in the preceding months. His testimony to the strength he had found there is eloquent.

It is only when one knows the ineffability of the Name of God that one can utter the name of Jesus Christ. It is only when one loves life and the world so much that without them everything would be gone, that one can believe in the resurrection and a new world. It is only when one submits to the law that one can speak of grace, and only when one sees the anger and wrath of God hanging like grim realities over the head of one's enemies that one can know something of what it means to love and forgive them.[6]

Without the Old Testament's sturdy stress on God's control of secular life, our preaching of the gospel would be emasculated. The preaching of a gospel of grace apart from its implementation in secular affairs is a docetic perversion. It is ghostly spirituality without bodily habitation—which is no biblical spirituality at all! Here again, Bonhoeffer has the apt word: "The Church stands not where human powers give out, on the borders, but in the center of the village. That is the way it is in the Old Testament and in this sense we still read the New Testament far too little on the basis of the

[6] *Letters and Papers from Prison* (paperback ed.; New York: The Macmillan Company, 1962), p. 103.

Old." [7] For in the Old Testament God's law is never confined to temple rites but stands dominant "in the centre of the village," controlling family life, rebuking commerce, regulating the trades, binding both kings and commoners with iron obligations, and making and unmaking governments in terms of their responses to its claims.

Preaching is under mandate to disturb men into seeing in this light our current struggles with culture. Failing that, we are left with a social relativity in which distinctions are lost and our road signs come down. "Segregation and integration are two types of culture," some men assert, "and you can be a Christian in either of them." [8] The Old Testament knows no such cultural neutrality! Before God, cultures do not stand on a dead level. Between Israel's desert culture and the culture of Canaan, issues of eternal moment are joined. A man must choose, and in the choice he is addressed by the Word. In the clash of cultures there are times when neutrality is betrayal. The silent man is the ally of injustice.

J. Wallace Hamilton makes this painfully clear in a sermon on the social relevance of Elijah's famous challenge: "How long will you go limping with two different opinions? If the Lord is God, follow him; but if Baal, then follow him" (I Kings 18:21). Baalism was more than a theological system; it was "an economic, political system—what we might call an ideology—a way of life," Dr. Hamilton points out.

[7] *Ibid.*, p. 166.
[8] Quoted by Joseph Ellwanger in "God's Plan: To Unite All Things in Christ" in *The Pulpit Speaks on Race,* Alfred T. Davies, ed. (Nashville: Abingdon Press, 1965), p. 41.

It grew out of an attitude towards property, the ownership of land. The word *baal* means "owner" and in the beginning it had nothing to do with religion. A slave's master was called a baal; a prince who controlled a fortified city or had large land holdings was called a baal; . . . a woman's husband was called her baal, her owner. Gradually the word came to be synonymous with the aristocracy, the upper classes who owned the land, . . . and had slaves to do their work for them. It came to be a religion when the land-owning artistocracy needed supernatural sanction to support their system and invented a god to fit it. They got the idea across that Baal was the god of fertility, good crops, and prosperity.[9]

Hebrew faith challenged this cultural system in the name of a religion whose expression ran all through secular society. "Not ownership but stewardship," Dr. Hamilton observes, integrated their life.

Authority was vested not in princes but in God. . . . He was the Owner, the Baal, and the earth was the Lord's. A land-holding aristocracy was prohibited by the Laws of Moses. The land-owner was only a tenant, holding his land in trust, and his lease on the land expired every fifty years (the year of Jubilee). His taxes were paid not to an earthly baal but to God—one tenth, a tithe of his production, administered by the priests.

No class distinctions were allowed in Israel. . . . It was a way of life in which the rights of man were safeguarded.[10]

Elijah called to nothing less than a choice between two whole cultures, two ways of life. He utterly repudiated the

[9] *The Thunder of Bare Feet* (Westwood, N. J.: Fleming H. Revell Company, 1964), p. 16.
[10] *Ibid.*, p. 17.

158

notion of cultural neutrality adopted on the assumption that faith is individualistic and other-worldly, independent of the secular order. The summons to this practical choice rings throughout the notable sermon with which Dr. Hamilton opens the series on *The Thunder of Bare Feet*.

In its first section it graphically documents the assertion that "These two contrasting philosophies have come down through history." [11] Against this background it declares second, that "like Elijah, we must face the painful truth: the old gods are hard to kill." [12] In a quick global tour it reviews the current struggle. Section three shows that "Within our lifetime we have known some brand-new names for Baalism." [13] As champion of the master *race,* it was known as fascism or nazism. When it made dominant a master *class,* it was called communism. It confronts us now in those who would turn us back from democracy's unfinished business in America and "in the hopes of people everywhere who are trying to shake off the shackles of the past!" [14] "The man or nation who would be master in the world must learn how to be the servant. The man in the castle must bow now to the Man born in a stable." [15]

One struggle fills the biblical scene, New Testament as well as Old—the clash of God's Word, through his mighty, saving acts, with the kingdom of evil. In the cross and resurrection of Jesus the decisive battle is fought, but the war does not end. All men are called to their part in this warfare. If it is a real and not a sham war, the outcome is in the

[11] *Ibid.,* p. 18.
[12] *Ibid.,* p. 22.
[13] *Ibid.,* p. 26.
[14] *Ibid.,* p. 28.
[15] *Ibid.,* p. 29.

balance in every engagement. Christ has won the crucial battle. His power has proven superior to the worst that evil can hurl against him. But we have been set at our battle posts; obedience is required of us.

We live by grace; we gladly preach grace. But we preach it amiss if we do not sound the note enunciated by John as the very first of all the signs: that the wonder wrought by Jesus does not set aside, but rather fills to the brim, the receptacle of the law. The Word interprets our life when it gives a full hearing to the Old Testament, read now in the light of the Cross, to be sure, but read by men of conscience for whom law is structural to life.

LIGHT ON THE FAITH WE PROCLAIM

Christian preaching of the Old Testament finds its climactic aid in the truth that we are men sent to proclaim a gospel whose meaning is lighted up by the ancient promises. "The prophecies are fulfilled," declared the New Testament preachers, "and the new Age is inaugurated by the coming of Christ." [16] The Old Testament reaches forward expectantly to a new age that is yet to be. Of that age the prophecies of a new covenant and the hope of the messianic era are dramatic harbingers, yet concerning it they cannot speak the final word. There is incompleteness yearning for fulfillment, bondage crying for deliverance. "Continuity here obviously cannot be analogous to the smooth continuity of water and milk," wrote Carl Michalson. "The relation is not so homogeneous. Nor is it, on the other hand, as discontinuous as water and oil. The relation is not so dichotomous. It is a

[16] *The Apostolic Preaching and Its Developments,* by C. H. Dodd (New York: Harper & Row, 1936), p. 17.

continuity, however, such as exists between thirst and water." [17]

"Christian faith takes the Old Testament words that were addressed to others and hears them spoken to itself." [18] Prophecy, spoken once to its own time and to a chosen people, speaks now to every time and to all people. The law helps us see the binding nature of the responsibilities within which we stand. God's call of Israel as his people guides the church's understanding of itself as the new Israel, called to go on mission as the people of God. Israel's salvation history becomes the story of our life.

The old covenant is founded on an understanding of human existence which is also basic to the gospel. It sees man, the creature of God and living under the divine command, yet a rebel against God's demand for obedience. It perceives the profound human need for the forgiveness and grace of God, if man is to escape from the threat of death under which his rebellion has placed him. . . . The Christian holds the Old Testament up as a mirror and sees in its understanding of the human predicament the reflection of his own face. [19]

The shocking aptness with which these ancient documents perform this interpretative function is seen in J. Elliott Corbett's application of the method of double analysis of biblical text and current scene to the Servant poem in Isaiah 52:14-53:12.

> *His appearance was so marred,*
> *beyond human semblance.*

[17] "Bultmann Against Marcion," in *The Old Testament and Christian Faith,* p. 60.
[18] *The Old Testament in Christian Preaching,* by Lawrence E. Tombs (Philadelphia: The Westminster Press, 1961), p. 26.
[19] *Ibid.*

Is it a man?
  His blood flows red,
  his tears are salty,
  his sweat runs down.
He had no form or comeliness
that we should look at him.
  His nose was too broad,
  lips too thick,
  hair too curly.
And no beauty that we should desire him.
  Would you want your daughter to marry one?
He was despised and rejected by men.
  He knew a door, not as an entranceway,
    but as a barrier to be shut in one's face:
    "Exclusive subdivision";
    "Private swimming club";
    "We reserve the right to choose our guests";
    "Opportunities for ambitious junior executives."
A man of sorrows,
  he sang comforting spirituals,
  finding his solace in an understanding God
  who alone knew the trouble he'd seen.[20]

Is this identification of the Servant fantastic? Not when one sees the Servant poem as written among the exiles in Babylon—defeated and captive nobodies, scorned by the society in which they held their second-class citizenship, who recognized themselves in the figure by which the prophet addressed them: "you worm Jacob, you men of Israel!" (Isa. 41:14). When we Christians see in the poem an incredibly apt delineation of our Lord, the scene is the Cross, where he

[20] *The Prophets on Main Street* (Richmond: John Knox Press, 1965), pp. 150-51.

162

hangs precisely because he too is a nobody whom the leaders of his society can scorn and the Roman overlord can treat as contemptibly expendable. It is just when the poem speaks in these shocking terms that hold the mirror to our relations with excluded people, that we see most truly what it is saying about God's Servant—in the Exile or on the Cross. Corbett keeps the image before us, line by line, coming at last to a shuddering conclusion:

> *Yet he bore the sin of many,*
>> twenty per cent without Caucasian blood.
>> "Separate but equal" equals unequal.
>> "The last to be hired, the first fired."
>> "The right to live next door—to somebody else."
> They gathered in the house of God
> *and made intercession for the transgressors,*
>> lifting prayers with hearts and voices,
>> hearts fervent, voices shrill,
>> "Ku Klux Klan," "Citizens Council,"
>> "Do not lay their sins against
>> who by our struggle are incensed." [21]

Through such stereoscopic vision the Old Testament becomes a vital interpreter of the faith we are charged to proclaim.

The preaching of the apostles, having opened with this note of prophecy fulfilled and God's new age begun, went on to declare that Jesus "was born of the seed of David." [22] Israel's history moved on in him. The struggle joined in its

[21] *Ibid.,* p. 152.
[22] Dodd, *The Apostolic Preaching and Its Developments,* p .17.

great epochs was part and parcel of the warfare he carried to victory. To catch the message of his messiahship, or to enter into the crucial decisions pivotal to his ministry, one must have light from the thought and events of the Old Testament.

It is not accidental that, for the decisive Sunday which ushers in Holy Week, Christians of many communions turn to the same Old Testament lesson; for Zechariah 9:9-12 is not only quoted in the Gospel accounts of the triumphal entry; it supplies indispensable background for the interpretation of the issues at stake.[23] Dealing with this Scripture, the interpreter may say:

We begin Holy Week with the claim that the cross erected before this week is done holds a king. But what kind of king? Matthew answered that question by appeal to this passage. In it a writer of Israel's postexilic period, whose work is preserved in the book of Zechariah, meditated on the messiah who would one day come. Jesus seems to have found these ideas helpful in his own thinking. At any rate, he appropriated the symbols as he entered Jerusalem. Having been important to the thinking of the church from the beginning—significant even for our Lord—this commanding conception speaks now to us.

Before we see in it Christ the King, we need to see the king hailed by the prophet. Clearly he spoke to the people of his time concerning their wistfully awaited new David, to whom they looked for the messianic reestablishment of the national

[23] Zech. 9:9-12 is cited in the Protestant Episcopal *Book of Common Prayer,* the Lutheran *Service Book,* the United Presbyterian, U.S.A. *Book of Common Worship,* and the *Book of Worship* of The Methodist Church—to name but a few.

throne. Yet this postexilic poet saw the coming one as no warrior. "Humble," he would come not on a horse of war but on a peasant's work animal. This was the more striking, since these lines may well have been written while Alexander the Great was sweeping everything before him. When such conquerors are gone and forgotten, he declared, another will come.

> I will cut off the chariot from Ephraim
>   and the war horse from Jerusalem;
> and the battle bow shall be cut off,
>   and he shall command peace to the nations.
>   (Zech. 9:10.)

Not everyone in Israel—any more than we who trust in arms now—accepted that estimate of the matter. The revolutionary party of the Zealots, represented even among Jesus' twelve disciples, pressed him to lead their armed uprising. On at least one occasion they tried to force his hand and make him king. When he refused, many turned from him as a useless dreamer. Bitter with such disappointed hopes, Judas may have planned his traitor's plot to salvage what he could. Jesus made his hard choice against this background.

Having seen the king hailed by the prophet, we can better see the king who comes in Jesus. He fought a battle no less real than any conquering king. In him the forces of God met the forces of evil in ultimate combat. His weapons, however, were of another kind. His battle with disease was part of that warfare. His choice of the known sinners in preference to the obviously righteous was no sentimental gesture; in his companionship with them he fought a battle to liberate them from the sins that enslaved them. When he sharpened issues so uncompromisingly that it cost crucifixion, his death on the cross was the climax of that battle. When God raised him from the dead, that set the seal of victory on the struggle. His death was no accidental martyrdom but the essence of his royal power. In his march to the cross he could not *know* that it would be so, but, walking by faith, as we must, he believed that God spoke through the prophet's word concerning this servant king:

> his dominion shall be from sea to sea,
> and from the River to the ends of the earth
> (Zech. 9:10).

The fact that today, after these centuries, a world-circling fellowship still faithful to him reaches out and takes us in testifies that it was so.

Today we see in him the king who calls his church to allegiance. The issue he had to decide—What *kind* of power is kingly?—remains pertinent. The choice is still being made. Such a disciple as Martin Luther King confronts us with it, not only in the choice between justice and flagrant injustice in the racial conflict, but in the choice of *means* to the ends we believe to be right. The old choice meets us in up-to-date form as the disinherited say to their most bitter opponents:

We shall match your capacity to inflict suffering by our capacity to endure suffering. We shall meet your physical force with soul force. Do to us what you will, and we shall continue to love you. We cannot in all good conscience obey your unjust laws, because nonco-operation with evil is as much a moral ob-

166

ligation as is co-operation with good. . . . Be ye assured that we will wear you down by our capacity to suffer. One day we shall win freedom, but not only for ourselves. We shall so appeal to your heart and conscience that we shall win *you* in the process, and our victory will be a double victory.[24]

Such choice, not only of ends but of means, represents the spirit of the Christ we hail on Palm Sunday, as he confronts the issues of our age. To be his disciples is to extend his spirit in the world. It is to carry on a battle against entrenched evil. It is to struggle by methods that serve peace in a time of strife.

In this hasty examination we have seen two affirmations of the New Testament preaching—the dawn of the new age of God's fulfillment, and the coming of Jesus as the crowning of Israel's hope—show their heightened color as the light of the Old Testament falls upon them. It would be possible to show that the same is true of the rest of the apostolic proclamation, but further detail is needless.

"He died according to the Scriptures, to deliver us out of the present evil age," [25] the apostles declared. They were speaking starkly of an event as local and datable as any item in today's news. Yet it became Word to them as rich overtones echoed through it, vibrating in tune with the deliverance of Israel in the Exodus, the restoration that followed Exile, the cleansing they had known in the sacrifice of the Day of Atonement, the liberation purchased by the Suffering

[24] Martin Luther King, *Strength to Love* (New York: Harper & Row, 1963), p. 40.
[25] Dodd, *The Apostolic Preaching and Its Developments*, p. 17.

Servant who "bore the sin of many." In the light of all these they better understood the Cross.

"He rose on the third day according to the Scriptures," [26] the New Testament preachers continued; and their phrase, "according to the Scriptures," winged the mind back from Easter's incredibly good news to such high hours as that of Ezekiel's vision of a valley of dry bones stirred to life as the promise of what God could do with a nation dead in its sinfulness.

"He will come again as Judge and Saviour of men," [27] their message continued, and that hope is never so triumphantly rich in meaning as when its terms are freighted with Old Testament recollections of the God who *comes,* of the *judgments* of God that are not only beyond history but in it, and of the glorious truth that our Redeemer is not one who intervenes between us and God but is none other than God himself. Because he is a God who *comes,* we expect to meet Christ in life's crises and judgments.

Christian dialogue with the Old Testament, recognizing that these pre-Christian documents must be heard in their own voice, comes to a realization that in them we have an authentic encounter with the Word of God. When we read them as Christians they interpret our life. When we read them as men of conscience they show us law as structural to our life. When we read them as men on mission with a faith to proclaim they show us depths of meaning we should otherwise have missed. But if the Old Testament thus aids us in encountering Christ, it is also true that wherever we go—in the Bible, or in our preaching, or in all the world—

[26] *Ibid.*
[27] *Ibid.*

Christ holds the key to the interpretations that finally show us who we are and what our life can mean. To explore this truth in terms of some of its specifics is the task of our final chapter.

For Further Study

1. *The Old Testament and Christian Faith,* a symposium edited by Bernhard W. Anderson (New York: Harper & Row, 1963) deals vigorously with the underlying problems at stake in this chapter. The central issue of the meaning of the Cross in the prespectives of both Testaments is taken up in two helpful books, *The Cross in the Old Testament,* by H. Wheeler Robinson (Philadelphia: The Westminster Press, 1956) and *The Old Testament in the Cross,* by J. A. Sanders (New York: Harper & Row, 1961). There is fine insight on the homiletic concerns at stake, in *The Old Testament in Christian Preaching,* by Lawrence E. Toombs (Philadelphia: The Westminster Press, 1961).

2. The lectionary of any major denomination selects Old Testament lessons for the Sundays of the year with careful attention to their relation to the message of the season and to their background support of the gospel. To practice the art of preaching from the Old Testament, turn to the lectionary for the season immediately following your reading of this book and prepare at least a sermon or two based on its Old Testament lessons. Robert C. Dentan, in *The King and His Cross* (New York: Seabury Press, 1965), shows what can be done with the lessons given in *The Book of Common*

Prayer for the days of Holy Week. Although his treatments are exegetical essays, not sermons, they help point a direction for your work. Or see the comments on two passages, pp. 151-53 and 165-68 above, which owe much to Dentan's studies.

7

Centered in the Word Incarnate

FINDING "GOSPEL" IN A TEXT

"Tell us what the good news is!" That direct plea
came from a nuclear physicist who had been introducing a
group of visiting theologians to his research. In the question
period one visitor asked: "How can religious leaders speak
more adequately to men living in the sophisticated world you
have been describing?" After his terse sentence response, the
scientist continued: "I go to church with some regularity.
There I hear frequent mention of some good news we
Christians are supposed to have. What is this news? We
need to hear, not talk about it, but the news itself."

This challenge, from an urbane leader of the atomic age, needs to be taken seriously. Not all religious discussion of current topics either *is* or *contains* a report of the good news. It is possible to speak with learning and eloquence, on themes both timely and pious, without making clear the news at the heart of the gospel. One can speak on a Bible passage with diligence that resolutely "sticks to the text," yet allow the good news to be so eclipsed by historical examination of the past event on the one hand, or moralistic exhortation on the other, that the good news never comes clearly in view. Yet, either from the vantage point of the New Testament or that of the nuclear age, reporting the good news is the preacher's first obligation.

When Walt Whitman spoke of finding letters from God dropped daily in the street, he doubtless thought more of what we now call "natural theology" than of biblical interpretation. Yet the personal letter's quality of direct address is so dominant in the Bible that the interpreter never speaks with the text's own accent unless men hear in it God's Word sent personally to them. This occurs, as the foregoing chapters have stressed, where text and listener meet in Christian tension and encounter within the framework of the present situation. The need for *Christian* encounter cannot be too strongly stressed. The Word becomes incarnate in Jesus Christ; to hear the Word is to meet *him*.

Preaching Christ is not a simple, one-step movement from every text to the gospel message, as chapter 6 has pointed out. Anxious haste to arrive too quickly at Christ may obscure the Word. When the interperter attempts, by typology or allegory, to prod a text which he deems too slow into yielding some immediate word of Christ, he is left without

172

real scriptural authority. For he has *made* the text say what, on other grounds, he believes it *ought* to say, and has not patiently listened to what it *does* say. Such preaching, at best, is left with no better authority than the preacher's common sense coupled with some knowledge of Christ gleaned from other sources than the text he purports to present.

Theologically such preaching is a wasted opportunity, having missed the true insight that remains locked in the passage. Morally it is dishonest, having shirked the effort to understand the specific text for the easier business of using it as pretext for the repetition of a general impression of a Christian point of view. Which is to say it has shortchanged both the listener and the gospel. Communicatively it fails, leaving thoughtful men with the uneasy feeling that, if this text comes from serious literature, there must be more in it than this too facile message has brought out.

How can preaching be delivered from these pitfalls? From "we must" preaching that neglects the good news for exhortation? From topical discussion that treats a subject but does not deliver the good news? From textual detail of what *has* happened, too preoccupied with past history to see its *current* news? From missing the real news in the text by torturing from it a forced allusion to Christ, instead of hearing the more specific truth it speaks in its own right? The good news is Christ; to interpret the text truly is to discover how it leads to him. But what does this mean? How is it done dependably and responsibly? How does the preacher meet this primary demand of his calling?

To answer these questions fully would require a retracing of every major discipline of theology and biblical study, for this is their ruling purpose. A single chapter can offer only some key suggestions, but it would be unthinkable to conclude a consideration of the interpreting Word without attempting that much.

IN CHRIST LAW MEETS GRACE

Let us say, first, that to find Christ's good news in the text is to be attentive to its word of law and grace as they meet in him. Eduard Thurneysen's study of *The Sermon on the Mount* [1] is instructive in this regard. Its approach to this one body of teaching is richly suggestive of a fruitful way of listening to much else in the Scriptures.

The Christ of the Sermon on the Mount is the giver of a demanding law. Matthew seems to have had this in mind as he adopted the literary pattern for his Gospel, structuring it around five extended discourses as a kind of Christian Torah. Our preaching on texts from this sermon easily falls into legalistic ways of thinking about *what we must do,* what our Lord *demands* of us. Interpretation which remains in this orbit requires the impossible. Thurneysen sees the claim this sermon lays upon us as resembling a cliff a mile high which stands in the way of a mountain climber. To go no further than the opening chapter, see its demands: Reconciliation with one's brother that goes to the core of one's inner attitude (Matt. 5:21-26), absolute purity not only in act but in heart (vss. 27-32), plain truthfulness that makes one's word one's bond (vss. 33-37), magnanimity that goes the second mile and turns the other cheek (vss. 38-47),

---

[1] (Paperback ed.; Richmond: John Knox Press, 1964). The approach to this section is drawn in general from this provocative and incisive book, though Thurneysen is not responsible for my way of developing his thesis —or my departures from it.

174

capped by perfection "as your heavenly Father is perfect" (vs. 48). Who can scale this "mile high cliff"?

Legalistic interpretation of these demands plunges us into frustration. Is Jesus, who quarrelled with the legalism of the Pharisees, compounding the problem by driving legalistic demands to the inner core of our being? Is he who "knew what was in man" (John 2:25) requiring of us what no man can deliver? Is he not rather describing the symptoms of the presence of the kingdom of God? Where these qualities appear, God is at work; his reign has begun. The Sermon deals with the kingdom from the moment its opening words are spoken. "Blessed are the poor in spirit, for theirs is the kingdom of heaven." (Matt. 5:3.) This is the keynote; this sets the theme. Those who are "comforted," who "inherit the earth," who are "satisfied"; those who "obtain mercy," "see God," or are "called the sons of God," are manifestly those whom God has helped. He has made them his own. They live under his reign. They are not absolved from their own response to him, but their new life is not the achievement of their endeavor. This truth of the Beatitudes indicates the intent of all the rest: throughout the Sermon Jesus is declaring the good news of the new life God gives within his kingdom.

How does he give it? First of all, in Jesus, who is not only the Lawgiver but the Doer. He fulfills the law (Matt. 5:17) and goes beyond it to demand a better righteousness than that of the scribes and Pharisees (vs. 20). What he asks—even at this impossible level—he delivers. For though the Sermon on the Mount can be said to describe the actual life of no one else, it is undeniably *descriptive of him.* "Unless your righteousness exceeds that of the scribes and Pharisees, you

175

will never enter the kingdom of heaven" (vs. 20)—what a frightening judgment! But there is one ray of hope in it; the kingdom of heaven already lives in Christ.

See him at the culminating hour of his life, as the battle is fought to its decisive issue on the cross. Such an end could not be improvised; it makes visible in a climactic moment what has been implicit in the quality of his whole life. In the fierce light that shines on that terrible hilltop, what we see from beginning to end is the fulfillment of all that, in the Sermon, he had taught.

He laid down the exacting requirement that we forgive our brother (Matt. 6:14-15) and pray for those who persecute us (Matt. 5:44); and the first word we hear from Calvary is his prayer of forgiveness: "Father, forgive them; for they know not what they do" (Luke 23:34). He promised the kingdom of heaven to the poor in spirit (Matt. 5:3); and from the cross we hear him assure the criminal who confessed his poverty: "Truly, I say to you, today you will be with me in Paradise" (Luke 23:43). He required that we keep all the law, relaxing none of it (Matt. 5:17-19)— which included the law of reverence and provision for parents; and even in his supreme agony he remembered to provide for his mother: "Woman, behold your son! . . . Behold your mother!" (John 19:26-27). He blessed those who hunger and thirst for righteousness (Matt. 5:6); and we hear his yearning not only for water, but also for the fulfillment of God's righteousness, in his famished cry: "I thirst" (John 19:28). He declared the impossibility of serving two masters (Matt. 6:24); and on the cross he held firmly to his single-minded service of God, even in the dark hour which tore from his throat the cry: "My God, my God, why hast thou forsaken me?" (Mark 15:34). He called us to enter by a narrow gate, since those who find life are few (Matt. 7:13-14); and he so followed that narrow way to its embattled end that he could die with the victor's shout: "It is finished" (John 19:30). He enjoined us not to be anxious about our life under any of its troubled conditions, since God knows our need and will provide for those who seek his kingdom (Matt. 6:25-34); and when life pressed him to his last agonizing breath, the final sound we hear from Calvary is the note of his trust: "Father, into thy hands I commit my spirit!" (Luke 23:46). What he asked of us on the Mount of the Sermon, he himself lived to the final extremity on the Mount of the Cross.[2] He who sets before us the "mile high wall" himself scaled it.

As the Doer of this demanding law, he accepts us who continually fall short. "I came not to call the righteous, but sinners" (Matt. 9:13), he said, accepting us in all our failure. Nor was the acceptance idle sentimentality, for he made of forgiveness the means of liberation from our sinfulness. Knowing our proneness to failure and our repeated falls, he taught us when we pray to say, "Forgive us our debts" (Matt. 6:12). Knowing our poverty of spirit, unable to win our own way into God's favor, he yet promised us the kingdom of heaven (Matt. 5:3). In one beatitude after an-

[2] The idea in this paragraph grew out of a swift suggestion dropped by James T. Cleland in personal conversation, concerning a series of sermons he had worked out, showing that in the Words from the Cross Jesus put in practice the teachings strewn across his ministry. These sermons have since been published in Professor Cleland's book, *He Died As He Lived* (Nashville: Abingdon Press, 1965). I am grateful to Professor Cleland for the insight, and can only wish I might have had access to the wisdom of his book—which had not yet appeared—in the writing of this passage.

other he made promises to those who cannot achieve in their own right. This is true even of those who "hunger and thirst after righteousness," for on the Semitic ears which first heard the Sermon, the word "righteousness" would fall with overtones of God's "vindication," "deliverance," "salvation." Those who "hunger and thirst after righteousness," Rudolph Bultmann observes, obviously are not "those who, 'ever striving, endeavor' to attain ethical perfection, but those who long to have God pronounce the verdict 'righteous' as his decision over them in the judgment." [3] The Beatitudes, keynoting the Sermon on the Mount, reflect his whole life's attitude as one of acceptance of those who struggle and fall short.

What blessed good news! *He who gives the law and in himself perfectly fulfills its demands, thus embodying the kingdom he describes, accepts us!* Yet he does not condone our failure or our sin. Even while he accepts us, he holds that same high expectation before us; for in the last moments of the Sermon on the Mount he sets us once more before that "mile high wall." "Not every one who says to me, 'Lord, Lord,' shall enter the kingdom of heaven, but he who does the will of my Father who is in heaven." (Matt. 7:21.) Now, however, the demand no longer frustrates; for by his acceptance we have been given a new power and motivation, a new freedom from anxiety and from self, to address ourselves to it. His acceptance, seen in all his life and supremely in the Cross, is our liberation.

The Cross shows the power of forgiveness, not to cancel the law but to fulfill it. However much we may boast that we need no forgiveness—can manage our own mistakes and want

---

[3] Quoted by Thurneysen, *The Sermon on the Mount*, p. 7.

no riding in on another's coattails—the Cross sobers us and shows us that forgiveness is necessary. For the very sins in which we are engulfed did this ultimate wrong. In the men and women who brought this monstrous deed to pass we see ourselves—in the Pharisees our self-righteousness and religious divisiveness; in the Sadducees our cultural pride conforming us to the spirit of the age, in conflict with the Spirit of our Lord; in Pilate's vacillations our irresolute wavering between personal conviction and fear of censure; in the sins of the outcasts he had befriended, though it outraged the orthodox, our own sinfulness.

This new understanding of who we are in our sinfulness, seeing our sins in a new light and so facing in a new direction, is the essence of repentance. It opens the way to forgiveness, which is not cancellation of consequences but restoration of relationship; when we *see* and *turn* in a new direction, we are again with him who had been seeing in this light and going this way all along. So the grace given on the Cross restores us to harmony with God and his law.

The Cross shows us in what ultimate regard the forgiving God holds the law. He does not lightly set it aside. His forgiveness is not casual and easy. He takes sin seriously. His forgiveness is not offered in order that we may go on our unrepentant way in blithe disregard of his commands. He forgives us because forgiveness itself is the most healing, correcting power in all the world.

> He died that we might be forgiven,
> he died to make us good.[4]

[4] Cecil F. Alexander, "There Is a Green Hill Far Away."

And the grace given on the Cross imparts redoubled motives and new power to live by the law that once defeated us.

The Cross shows us that, no matter how desperately we have transgressed the law, forgiveness is possible for us. No man need wistfully say: "Forgiveness is for others, but not for me; God's pardon is beyond my reach." For the Cross shows that no man is beyond God's reach. Every desperate sin that drove Jesus to his cross was covered in his prayer for God's forgiveness. In his death evil flung against him every weapon in its arsenal; but in his resurrection he showed how impotent all the powers of evil were to defeat God's goodness. He won a battle against the whole kingdom of evil, which includes the farthest, most desperate guilt into which any one of us can fall. In his resurrection appearances he sought out those who had doubted and denied him and restored them by his forgiveness—as the living Christ continues to do. He lives on in his body, the church, and in that redeeming fellowship forgiveness is ours. We can experience forgiveness within ourselves and know its peace, and the experience is no subjective illusion. As Paul said: "When we cry, 'Abba! Father!' it is the Spirit himself bearing witness with our spirit that we are children of God" (Rom. 8:15-16). That assurance releases new powers within us to live as God's children, in harmony with his will for us. As Paul again put it: "I press on to make it my own, because Christ Jesus has made me his own" (Phil. 3:12).[5]

What confronts us, as from the foot of the Cross we hear

[5] For a fuller development of the thought in the three foregoing paragraphs cf. James S. Stewart, *A Faith to Proclaim* (New York: Charles Scribner's Sons, 1953), pp. 48-75.

our Lord in the Sermon on the Mount, meets us wherever we go in the Scriptures. He who gives the law fulfills it—first in himself and then, by his acceptance, in us who were at odds with it. To find the *gospel* in a passage, one must look for the way in which it reveals *that* taking place. Here, for instance, is the story of the sick man who said to Jesus, "Sir, I have no man to put me into the pool when the water is troubled, and while I am going another steps down before me"; to whom our Lord replied: "Rise, take up your pallet, and walk" (John 5:7-8). How does one preach from such a text?

One approach is that of the sharp eye for ethical concern. The man had been there for thirty-eight years, the preacher notes, and no one helped him. Yet Jesus observed him there and healed him. The man could say, "I have no man to help me"—but only until Jesus passed that way. How many people like that are all around us! No one notices them. They can say with true pathos, "I have no man to help me." That cry is multiplied by the thousands, day after day. But that is what Christians are in the world for! What our Lord did, we must do. As he noted and helped the forgotten, so must we. Such an approach to the text has ethical virility, which we may be sure is dear to the heart of our Lord; yet the note of the good news is smothered by the demand. The gospel has been engulfed in the law.

There is an alternative approach which notes how like this sick man we are. We are paralyzed, crippled, less than we could have been. Old sins, buried guilt, defeating tensions have us in their grip. Much as we yearn to be more than we are—not only for our own sakes, but to be more joyfully

181

helpful to those we love—here we are among the invalids. There is even some question, after all these years, whether we have the will to be well; so that Jesus can ask us, as appropriately as he asked this man by the pool, "Do you want to be healed?" Like him, we are losing our capacity to take responsiblity for ourselves, looking around for someone else to lay it on: "I have no man to put me into the pool." But—wonder of wonders!—Jesus speaks the liberating word, and we can be healed. This approach is more hopeful, having found the good news. It is possible, however, that it may do so at the cost of the ethical strength shown in the first.

But the preacher can preserve the values of both approaches. He might begin much as the first preacher did, proceeding in a dialectical pattern: (a) All around us are the helpless, saying, "I have no man." We Christians are in the world to help them. (b) Yet we are powerless, for we too are crippled, preoccupied with our own trouble. (c) Christ releases us and sets us to the task of sharing his help with these others. This sermon design would preserve both law and gospel in a meaningful encounter with the good news.

Even closer to the structure of the passage itself might be a straight-line design which would say: (a) We see ourselves here by the pool, crippled as we are. (b) The wonder is that Christ releases us. (c) The forgiving love which released us sets us to following his command that we "Sin no more" (John 5:14), which calls us to obey God and help our brother even as Christ has helped us. Either of these structures can yield a sermon which validly conveys the wholeness of the Word in the passage, because in both, law and grace meet in Jesus Christ.

182

COVENANTS COALESCE IN CHRIST

A second key to the discovery of the good news in a passage lies in attentiveness to its relationship to both the old covenant and the new as they are embodied in Jesus Christ. Both are needed to interpret our life as we live it under God's call and promise. The unity of the Bible holds together in God's covenant relation with his people. "No more fruitful inquiry can be made than to search the Scriptures for light on the covenant idea." [6]

The covenant joined at Sinai was the creative center of Israel's life. It gave structure and cohesiveness to the community in its sense of mission, from which sprang the vitality of the law and the power of a people's purpose. It enjoined undivided loyalty (Deut. 4:23) and promised God's dependable faithfulness (Deut. 4:30-31). In this twofold movement is the heart of God's relations with men: with insistent claim and unyielding demand he calls, and with unfailing graciousness he keeps faith.

From this covenant bond grew the selfhood of Israel as a community of peculiar destiny and unique responsibility. Psalms 105, 106, and 107 celebrate in song what lies implicit in the whole structure of the common life: that Israel's emergence from bondage into nationhood was not her own doing but the gift of God, that the people's rebelliousness was a violation of a deep obligation to him, that because of their special relation to God they were judged by a sterner standard than any other people, and that despite their failures he restored them in merciful forgiveness.

[6] Otto J. Baab, *The Theology of the Old Testament* (Apex ed.; Nashville: Abingdon Press, 1949), p. 136.

> Many times he delivered them,
>> but they were rebellious in their purposes,
>> and were brought low through their iniquity.
> Nevertheless he regarded their distress,
>> when he heard their cry.
> He remembered for their sake his covenant,
>> and relented according to the abundance of his
>> steadfast love. (Ps. 106:43-45.)

The obstinate refusal of the prophets to move pliably with the mind of their time roots in this double movement of the covenant relation with God. When the popular mood was optimistic they prophesied doom, and when despair engulfed the people they proclaimed hope; for both exacting judgment and redeeming love were implicit in the way in which God had bound them to himself and himself to them. Israel's stern discipline, her unparalleled frankness in chronicling her sins, and her capacity to survive destructive catastrophe cannot be understood apart from this covenant relation.

Sinai's stance in history gave Israel a point of departure from which to interpret the meaning of life from its beginnings. The vitality imparted by what had happened under Moses and the prophets called for explanation, which was forthcoming in faith's appropriation of legendary prehistory. God, who had chosen Israel by a free choice, not explainable by any worthiness in this tiny people, had made the choice far earlier in his covenant with their father Abraham. Faith saw in the deliverance from Egypt a revealing "inner history." What had occurred at the Red Sea, in the wilderness wanderings and the arrival in the promised land—far from happenstance—was seen as a classic demonstration of God's dependable faithfulness.

184

Little wonder that faith took the further step of finding the covenant relation a basic condition of human existence, expressed in God's covenant with all men through Noah, sealed with the rainbow in the cloud: "never again shall all flesh be cut off by the waters of a flood, and never again shall there be a flood to destroy the earth" (Gen. 9:11). So, from the central fact of Israel's existence—the covenant made at Sinai—insight grew into the larger revelation of God's bond with all men.

Insights of continuing importance in interpreting us inhere in the covenant nature of our life. To live under a sense of *claim* upon us is the root of our humanity. The undiscovered and the unexplained lay their claim on curiosity, calling forth an articulate mind to compass the unknown. Life in community lays its claim on the latent sense of "oughtness," summoning conscience to awaken. Duty claims response to burdens which build fibre and deepen satisfaction even while they test us. Love binds with ties of responsible concern, but its captivity sets one free to become what apart form love's obligation he could not be: patient and kind; not jealous or boastful, arrogant or rude; not insisting on one's own way; not irritable or resentful; not rejoicing at wrong, but rejoicing in the right; bearing, believing, hoping, enduring all things (cf. I Cor. 13:4-7). Submitting to the claim, one becomes a man, giving up childish ways (vs. 11). Life's insistent claims stretch us into full humanity in response to a covenant woven into the warp and woof of our existence. All this is not impersonal, as if natural conditioning were its final explanation. It is not relative, a product of changing mores of successive societies. It is an I-Thou relation with God himself, fundamental to our existence, to

185

violate which is to betray him and to strike a blow at our own being.

Through the covenant we see our position of responsibility amid the destruction caused by sin. There is pertinence in God's colloquy with Noah as an ancient rabbinical commentary preserves the tradition. It pictures Noah in bitter tears as he stepped out of the ark and saw the ravages the flood had wrought. "O Lord of the world!" he cried, "Thou art called the Merciful, and Thou shouldest have had mercy upon Thy creatures." Whereupon God replied: "O you foolish shepherd, now you speak to Me. You did not do so when I addressed kind words to you, saying: 'I saw you as a righteous man and perfect in your generation, and I will bring the flood upon the earth to destroy all flesh.' " [7] The suggestion of Noah's tardy concern, and God's implication that an earlier prayer might have helped avert the catastrophe, reflects much in the human situation down to this day of crisis in which we stand. When rioting breaks out, or bombs fall, we cry out in complaint against God, unmindful of our neglected justice and violated covenant that have brought the catastrophe upon us.

Yet there is hope. It inheres in God's grace to those who return to him in faithfulness. For grace speaks through the Old Covenant as well as the New. God chose Israel of his own initiative, based on his love, not on her worthiness (Deut. 7:7-8). From Old Testament data Paul argued in Romans and Galatians that gospel had preceded law, not the reverse. It was by his grace that God gave the covenant, so that law

---

[7] Midrash on the book of Genesis. For this incisive quotation I am indebted to my friend and colleague, Rabbi David Polish.

itself is rooted in grace. Human righteousness can never match the righteousness of God.

Through the covenant we see the meaning in otherwise inexplicable tragedy. The great Isaiah of the Exile understood the suffering of his time as evidence that God was fulfilling his covenant by using exiled Israel as a servant through whom he would realize his universal purpose for the salvation of the nations. In the harsh experience God was saying:

> I have given you as a covenant to the people,
>   a light to the nations,
>   to open the eyes that are blind,
> to bring out the prisoners from the dungeon,
>   from the prison those who sit in darkness (Isa. 42:6-7).

Other nations, looking on, could say of the spiritual Israel:

> He was wounded for our transgressions, . . .
>   and with his stripes we are healed. . . .
> the Lord has laid on him the iniquity of us all (Isa. 53:5-6).

So, amid the reverses of the Exile, God was seen keeping his covenant and turning even this climactic evil to his own ends for the salvation of the peoples. Through Israel's experience we come to see that, even in our enforced sufferings, God can find the witness with which he ushers in a new day.

Even before the Exile, prophetic insight pointed forward to a new covenant. Trust in the letter, in the institution, called forth the answering faith of Jeremiah:

Behold, the days are coming, says the Lord, when I will make
a new covenant with the house of Israel and the house of Judah,
not like the covenant which I made with their fathers when I
took them by the hand to bring them out of the land of Egypt,
my covenant which they broke, though I was their husband, says
the Lord. But this is the covenant which I will make with the
house of Israel after those days, says the Lord: I will put my
law within them, and I will write it upon their hearts; and I
will be their God, and they shall be my people. And no longer
shall each man teach his neighbor and each his brother, saying,
"Know the Lord," for they shall all know me, from the least
of them to the greatest, says the Lord; for I will forgive their
iniqiuty, and I will remember their sin no more (31:31-34).

In the face of the tendency to make the covenant a matter of
legal observance which overshadowed the grace that gave
it, this emphasis classically stated in Jeremiah finds expression in a host of passages in Deutero-Isaiah (42:6; 49:8;
55:3; 61:8) and Ezekiel (34:25; 37:26).

What the prophets had foreseen, the New Testament
brought to flower. Luke incorporates the tradition in his
announcement of the gospel as he puts into the song of
Zechariah the assurance of God's purpose:

to perform the mercy promised to our fathers,
and to remember *his holy covenant,*
the oath which he swore to our father Abraham, to grant us
that we, being delivered from the hand of our enemies,
might serve him without fear,
in holiness and righteousness before him all the days of our
life (1:72-75, italics added).

Jesus made the new covenant imagery pivotal to the interpretation of his sacrifice. His words at the Last Supper

reveal his conviction that God would ratify a covenant with a new Israel through his death, even as he had sealed his covenant at Sinai with the blood of sacrificial animals. There Moses sprinkled the blood upon the people, saying, "Behold the blood of the covenant which the Lord has made with you" (Exod. 24:8). The parallel expressed by Jesus—"This is my blood of the covenant, which is poured out for many" (Mark 14:24)—is unmistakable. Though Moses' act seems repulsive by our standards, it was the way in which covenants were made in that period; and Jesus in the upper room made telling use of the symbolism to mark a new covenant which, according to Paul, he commanded his disciples to repeat in perpetual remembrance of him (I Cor. 11:25).

The writer to the Hebrews spells out the implications of this aspect of the mind of our Lord, making it central to his elaborate argument. Thus the covenant theme, spanning the Scriptures, binds them into a unity at whose summit are Christ and his cross-resurrection, the new exodus from the bondage of sin and death.

The search for the good news in any text involves the quest for its place within this overarching relationship to the old covenant and the new, as they meet in Jesus Christ. See, for example, how Joel 2:12-19, a lesson frequently cited in the lectionaries for Ash Wednesday, grows luminous within this perspective. Its call to penitent fasting looks back to the scourge of locusts as evidence of God's judgment. "The years which the swarming locust has eaten" (vs. 25)—years of depression, war, and such undisciplined living as reflects widespread erosion of conscience—recall us to our own violated covenant of obedience. Catastrophic events do not negate meaning in our life; their judgment confirms it. They press home the truth that we live under a claim and are called to full humanity.

Joel looked forward, as well as back, confident that God

> is gracious and merciful,
> slow to anger, and abounding in steadfast love,
> and repents of evil (vs. 13).

He is the God of the new covenant, whose ultimate judgment on our sin was rendered in the Cross by which he reconciles us to himself. He draws us into harmony by making us sure that we are completely accepted. Society accepts only the amiable "front" we present, as in the patient voice we manage to preserve through a trying conversation. With the receiver safely on the hook we mutter curses and imprecations. But God accepts both sides of our nature—the devout prayers and the raging temper. When our explosive self knows itself accepted, its grip on us is relaxed. We can laugh at ourselves, take ourselves less seriously, and to that degree be harmonized with the better self we aspire to become.[8]

Pivotal to our life within the covenant relation is our penitent return.

> "Yet even now," says the Lord,
>   "return to me with all your heart,
> with fasting, with weeping, and with mourning;

---

[8] Cf. H. A. Williams, *The True Wilderness* (Philadelphia: J. B. Lippincott Company, 1965), p. 147.

and rend your hearts and not your garments." (Joel
2:12-13a.)

The call is imperative as war inflames our passions. The
inner scar it leaves was revealed in the widely publicized
letter of a marine and the nationwide accolade of approval
it called forth. "You learn to hate real fast," wrote the young
lieutenant. "Not like you used to hate the bully at the end
of the block, or your boss, or that nosy next-door neighbor.
No, it's the kind of primitive hatred where you almost seem
to enjoy seeing an enemy's guts spilled onto the deck—or his
twisted, bloated body." [9] The letter then turned to a similar
hatred of comfortable Americans at home who question the
foreign policy which sends young men to such carnage.
Letters to the press, across the nation, revealed a storm
of violent emotion in civilian hearts not unlike that which
the heat of battle had built up in the young fighting man.

But if the military sacrifice is to have any possibility of
serving the intended welfare of Southeast Asia and the orderly life of the world community, or if the wake of the war
is not to be an America further rent by inner distrust and
explosive hatreds which will rend and cripple the national
life, such passions must be brought to heel. We need a new
covenant written on the heart. Penitence (*metanoia*), literally a new mind, calls for reexamination of our thought as
well as our deeds, to see where the areas we withhold from
God's sovereign control may lie. These blindnesses and re-
bellions have invited the locusts of moral and spiritual de-

---

[9] Letter of Lt. Ward Johnson, reported in the *Chicago Daily News,*
May 14, 1966.

struction, but, opened to God's reconciling love, they can lead into a future of restored hope.

GOD'S PEOPLE THROUGH CHRIST

Note one other key to the discovery of the good news in a passage—its relation to, or bearing on, the concept of the people of God into whose life we are incorporated through Jesus Christ. Law and grace, the old covenant and the new, find their place and meaning within this context. God chose this people as an expression of his love.

It was not because you were more in number than any other people that the Lord set his love upon you and chose you, for you were the fewest of all peoples; but it is because the Lord loves you, and is keeping the oath which he swore to your fathers, that the Lord has brought you out with a mighty hand, and redeemed you from the house of bondage. (Deut. 7:7-8.)

The dangers of the chosen-people concept are manifest. It adds a dimension of the demonic to the evils of racism. Arnold Toynbee alleges that this idea has made the nations of the West arrogant in their dealings with the other peoples of the earth. Why do thoughtful men suppose that a universal God makes a particular, localized people his "chosen"? Because his revelation comes to us not in generalizations but in the insights vouchsafed through historic events. And history moves with the tread of the local, the timely, the particular. Whatever happens in history must happen some*where,* some-*time,* in the affairs of some *people.* C. H. Dodd comments aptly on this scandal of particularity.

192

If in any given case we ask why this and not that, I do not see what account can be given of it except that the Ruler of the universe willed it so. He chose *this* time, *this* land, *this* people for the revelation of himself, and what it means is that no one must ever suppose that he belongs to the people of God through any achievement or merit of his own. Membership of God's people is *sola gratia,* and was never on any other terms." [10]

God's people are called to no privileged position. On the contrary, to belong to his people is to be judged by a more rigorous standard. His Word spoken through Amos is explicit:

> You only have I known
>   of all the families of the earth;
> therefore I will punish you
>   for all your iniquities (3:2).

God chose his people for mission. So deeply is this understanding imbedded in the Old Testament that as early as the covenant with Abraham it reads God's purpose that "by your descendants shall all the nations of the earth bless themselves, because you have obeyed my voice" (Gen. 22:18). In executing his choice at Sinai, God said to the people through Moses: "Now therefore, if you will obey my voice and keep my covenant, you shall be my own possession among all peoples; for all the earth is mine, and you shall be to me a kingdom of priests and a holy nation" (Exod. 19:5-6). In his concern for righteousness, the Isaiah of the Exile declared, God set Israel as a "light to the nations" (Isa. 42:6). The

[10] "The Biblical Doctrine of the People of God," in *The Doctrine of the Church,* Dow Kirkpatrick, ed. (Nashville: Abingdon Press, 1964), p. 31.

prophet was convinced, as we have seen, that God's way of using his people as a witness to the nations was to exact from them service through suffering.

Whoever sees in the concept of the people of God grounds for lording it over others, or for complacency within oneself, has not even begun to catch its meaning within the biblical record. Yet the pull of the notion of privilege is ever upon us. We justified releasing nuclear holocausts on Hiroshima and Nagasaki, and have since defended wanton cruelties in Viet Nam, by arguments which have special privilege as an unexpressed major premise: Horrible as it is, these victims must be immolated to save American lives; such suffering does not mean to these Asians, who have known only hardness and cruelty, what it means to us; the higher civilization of the West must be defended against the encroachment of other ways of life, even if fighting fire with fire means the ultimate destruction.

By such thinking we destroy our witness as God's people in the name of preferment and privilege. For our adoption of a lower standard of conduct in the name of expediency shows where our ultimate trust lies "when the chips are down." Albert Camus, professing to be outside the fold of Christ, may have seen with an outsider's objective clarity in reporting the remark of one of his characters on a wartime casualty. "When an innocent youth can have his eyes destroyed, a Christian should either lose his faith or consent to having his eyes destroyed." [11] That conviction was not far from Jesus' rule for his people: "Whoever would save his life will lose it; and whoever loses his life for my sake and the gospel's will save it" (Mark 8:35). To let the biblical text in-

[11] *The Plague* (New York: The Modern Library, 1948), p. 207.

194

terpert the meaning of our life at this point is a desperate need of the contemporary church.

Paul invoked the prophetic doctrine of the *remnant* in puzzling out the problem of the passing of the choice from Israel. Yet the thought of a righteous remnant was difficult to harmonize with the infant church, marked as it was by human frailty and sinfulness. To follow the thinking of C. H. Dodd again, Jesus' own words—"I came not to call the righteous, but sinners" (Matt. 9:13)—denied any special righteousness among those associated with him. He was known indeed as " a friend of tax collectors and sinners" (Matt. 11:19). Even on the cross he was hung between two criminals, and Paul dared to say that he died under the curse of the law. The charter members of this community of faith had deserted their Lord in the hour of his greatest crisis and could belong to him only by virtue of his forgiveness. "They were members of the People of God *sola gratia.*" [12]

Steadily the servant people had narrowed. Israel had not fulfilled the role, nor had a faithful remnant among the people made its appearance. If there had been any hope that the disciples whom Jesus gathered would play this part, their performance in his betrayal, their denials of him, and their flight from the cross had shattered it. In Christ alone was the remnant to be found. He only was the true Israel.

His church becomes the people of God through its corporate identification with him. Not of our own right can we belong to this people. But when we hear the Word of God spoken to us in him, when we repent and accept the new life he gives, we are incorporated into the new Israel and hold our membership *sola gratia.*

[12] "The Biblical Doctrine of the People of God," p. 35.

195

Only incorporation into Christ makes a church—not voluntary association, nor mutual agreement, nor liking for one another's company, nor idealistic desire to do good. "The church is the company of those who are in Christ, all believers, regardless of their political, economic, racial, or cultural ties. If we are in Christ we have no option; we are one with one another." [18] This is the controlling truth concerning church unity, or racial integration in the church, or the church's bridging of national or class lines. In fellowship with him we are in fellowship with one another; out of fellowship with one another we are out of fellowship with him; out of fellowship with him we are no longer his church.

To preach is to renew the call by which men are incorporated into him. Discussions *about* him are not equal to this task; men must needs hear *him*. It is our calling to bring his words, his acts, the insights he affords into such contact with the life we share with our people that they find themselves understood and interpreted. In this new knowledge of who they are and who they can be, they are brought to repentance and the new life in him. Our task is not to talk at secondhand *about* the good news, but to report the news itself.

Men need to hear the news that in Christ the requirements of God's law are fully met; and because he forgives us, we have a new and joyful freedom to be truly ourselves by giving ourselves up to him who made us, loves us, and can fulfill us. They need to hear the news that God keeps covenant with his people, not because we are great or worthy but because he is loving; and when we open ourselves to him in faith,

---

[18] Alvin M. Rogness, in *Preaching on Pentecost and Christian Unity,* Alton M. Motter, ed. (Philadelphia: Fortress Press, 1965), p. 223.

he so writes his law upon the deepest motives of our hearts that the changed climate of thought and emotion nurtures our growth into a kind of person we once despaired of being. They need to hear the news that, in spite of all our failure and sin, God calls us to live in communion with Christ, made one with the people of God, sent on mission to serve a lost world and to find our life fulfilled in giving it up to him and for the brothers for whom he died. They need to hear the news that God has won his warfare with evil; and though we have a battle post to hold at all costs, we can stand our ground and win the day, for the decisive engagement has been won, so that he who endures to the end shall be saved.

Varied Ministries—One Priority

The interpreter is commissioned not to summarize this message in broad and general terms, but to let each passage declare it in its own specific, concrete detail. Every passage has its own unique and authentic note to strike, yet each strikes it truly only when its good news centers in the Word incarnate. To live and work so attuned that he can detect that note, yet to be so much at the disposal of his people's need that he can enable them to hear it as the secret of their life, is the vital business to which God has called the preacher. Exciting business it is, and costly.

The cost may seem prohibitive. Who can manage the sheer investment of time required for such study as the interpreter's life demands? There is counseling to be done, there are calls to be made, a church school to man and administer, community relations to cultivate, a vital institution to maintain. Can one *also* preach as this concept of the interpreting Word requires? One can, and one must!

This is central. From this all else that transpires in church life and ministerial work derives its meaning. This Word calls the church into being. To convey this Word the church was sent on mission; around this Word it builds its life. Failing real encounter with this Word, it flattens out into one more human association, going through the motions of its old habitual functions with no inner life and no reason for being.

Can one *also* preach? To ask it so is to get everything wrong. There will be no right answers because the question is wrongly put. Can one be true to *any other* ministry if he is false to this ministry of the interpreting Word?

That conflict need not arise. These are not two ministries but one. The ministry of pastoral care, community service, education, administration brings its own contribution to the ministry of the Word. The preacher is the man of the Book, but he is more. For the Book alone is insufficient. It is God's dialogue with men and is heard aright only by one who lives among men, loves them, enters deeply into their life, and comes to the Book with them in his heart. As he studies it, he asks their questions, follows their escapes, feels the force of their doubts, agonizes with their griefs and guilt. A recluse cannot preach the interpreting Word, for he hears only one side of the dialogue and can decipher only snatches of its meaning. The option—ministry of parish activity *or* ministry of the Word—is not open to us. To choose either at the cost of the other is to destroy both.

If the minister of the Word must be much with people, he must not be *always* with them. Like his Lord, who loved men at the cost of his life yet left the Gospels strewn with the record of his withdrawals to be alone, the interpreter can make of his ministry what God intended only by disciplined use of time carefully guarded for the solitary study and meditation that are the essence of his calling. Some of this will come by lengthening his day, rising early to find clarity in his lone watch before the rush and interruptions of the day begin. Some will come by finding a solitary place of work—another office away from the one the public knows, a hideaway in the country, if nothing else a quiet place where he parks his car and gets in some solid hours of study and writing away from telephone and office. Some of it will come by diligent management of his time—no moment too fragmentary or unexpected to be used, because he has taken pains to see that a book and note materials are always at hand and always used when the available moment comes. Most of all, it will come because the passion of his life and his commitment to his Lord require it, no holiday happy without its hour of preparation of a better mind for the ministry. For this is his life; this is the basis of his integrity as a man called to the ministry of the Word and burning to be an honest workman at his craft. This is where his Lord has placed him, and here, at all costs, he will stand.

For Further Study

1. Eduard Thurneysen's argument in *The Sermon on the Mount* (paperback ed.; Richmond: John Knox Press, 1964) has been severely condensed as it entered into this chapter's discussion. It merits fuller attention and will repay careful reading and reflection. Christ's centrality in the Scriptures is, of course, the theme of many books; John Knox

celebrates it with special richness in *Life in Christ Jesus* (New York: Seabury Press, 1961). The Servant theme as related to the people of God is developed in detail in *Deutero-Isaiah, A Theological Commentary on Isaiah 40-55,* by George A. F. Knight (Nashville: Abingdon Press, 1965).

2. From your own study of John 5:2-14, together with your reflections on the suggested alternative treatments found on pp. 183-84 why not develop a sermon in which law and grace meet in Christ?

3. Taking Luke 3:10-18 as a typical passage in which, without explicit covenant language, the old and new covenants draw together, can you prepare a paragraph sermon which declares both aspects of the good news?

4. One of the most saving ways in which the Scriptures interpret us is by showing us our place in the people of God. Yet a balanced presentation of this theme is difficult to achieve. It would be helpful, against the background of the thought in pp. 193-98, to prepare a sermon on I Peter 1:4-10.

5. As we part, may I express the hope that you will continue some long-range concerns we have shared? Have you found a practice which gives you the values of the devotional diary? Are you incorporating in your pulpit planning at least some extended periods of preaching from the lectionary? Have you begun work on a Bible book course of sermons? Are you finding the freshness and power that come in using the varied patterns of interpretation we have studied? In your preliminary thinking about a text do you regularly let it examine and interpret *you?* Have you formed the habit of letting it enter into conversation with some of your people whom you have listed together with their current

needs of which you, as concerned pastor, are aware? If so, *your* interpretation of the text is beginning to turn into the *text's* interpretation of *us* as God's children. The text is becoming Word once more.

As you carry these concerns forward, may William Bright's prayer go with you:

O Lord Jesus Christ, who art the Truth incarnate and the Teacher of the faithful; let thy Spirit overshadow us in the reading of thy Word, and conform our thoughts to thy revelation; that learning of thee with honest hearts, we may be rooted and built up in thee, who livest and reignest with the Father and the Holy Spirit, world without end. Amen.

Index of Scripture

202

Index of Names and Subjects

205

Date Due